KS3
SCIENCE

SUMMARY BOOK

Brian Arnold

Hodder & Stoughton

A MEMBER OF THE HODDER HEADLINE GROUP

ACKNOWLEDGEMENTS

I would like to express my gratitude to the publishing team at Hodder & Stoughton Educational, especially Julia Morris and Charlotte Litt, who have offered invaluable advice throughout the project. Thanks also to the many friends and colleagues who gave so freely of their time, particularly towards the latter stages.

Finally, I would like to thank my wife Jill for her ever-present encouragement and patience. Without her support, there would have been no book.

Brian Arnold, 1999

The publishers would like to thank the following individuals, institutions and companies for permission to reproduce photographs in this book. Every effort has been made to trace ownership of copyright. The publishers would be happy to make arrangements with any copyright holder whom it has not been possible to contact.

Action-Plus Photographic (114 top), /Bruce Coleman Limited/Hans Reinhard (47 bottom), /Jane Burton (40 bottom left), /Jeff Foott Productions (46 left), /Jen & Des Bartlett (131 right), /John Cancalosi (41 bottom), /Jules Cowan (46 bottom right), /Kim Taylor (131 left), /Staffan Widstrand (51); Bubbles/Amanda Knapp (27 right), /Dr Hercules Robinson (27 left); Colin Taylor Productions (34, 41 top); Corbis (77 bottom), /Peter Turnley (14), /Richard Hamilton Smith (114 bottom); GSF Picture Library (77 top), /Imperial War Museum (28 left); Life File/Angela Maynard (81), /Emma Lee (47 top two, 80, 92 both), /Jeremy Hoare (50, 56, 116), /John Dakers (126), /Jon Woodhouse (84), /Mike Evans (46 top right), /Nigel Shuttleworth (68 top), /Richard Powers (76); Ping Golf Equipment (125); RD Battersby/Bo'sun Media Services (40 right); Science Photo Library/Alfred Pasieka (57 bottom), /Bruce Iverson (54), /Charles D Winters (99), /David Nunuk (139, 140 left), /David Parker (68 bottom), /David Taylor (57 top), /JC Teyssier (28 right), /Joe Tucciarone (140 right), /NASA (141 right), /PLI (136), /Rouxaime & Jacana (98), /Tony Craddock (149), /University of Dundee (141 top)

Orders: please contact Bookpoint Ltd, 39 Milton Park, Abingdon, Oxon OX14 4TD. Telephone: (44) 01235 400414, Fax: (44) 01235 400454. Lines are open from 9.00–6.00, Monday to Saturday, with a 24 hour message answering service. Email address: orders@bookpoint.co.uk

A catalogue record for this title is available from The British Library

ISBN 0 340 73077 3

First published 1999
Impression number   10   9   8   7   6   5   4   3   2
Year   2004   2003   2002   2001   2000   1999

Copyright © 1999 Brian Arnold

Cover photo from Bruce Coleman Ltd.
Illustrated by Tom Cross, William Donohoe, Richard Duszczak, Phil Ford, Ian Foulis & Associates, Peters & Zabransky (UK) Ltd.
Typeset by Wearset, Boldon, Tyne and Wear.
Printed in Great Britain for Hodder & Stoughton Educational, a division of Hodder Headline Plc, 338 Euston Road, London NW1 3BH by Scotprint, Musselburgh, Scotland.

CONTENTS

● STUDY SKILLS

Figure 1 Some people find it easy to study and actually enjoy learning! For others studying is not so easy. It is important that you find and use ways of studying that work for you

Listening

Listening is one of the most important study skills and yet it is one we often do badly. You can improve your listening skills by

◆ making a real effort to concentrate on every word when someone is explaining something.
◆ not getting distracted or letting your mind wander – this isn't easy but you will get better with practice.
◆ getting involved – asking questions, jotting down notes etc.

Making notes

It is likely that you will learn from your notes when it comes to revision time. It is, therefore, vital that you are able to read and understand them. It will help if you write them

◆ clearly
◆ in your own words
◆ in small manageable chunks.

Use lots of headings and short paragraphs as these kind of notes are easy to dip into for information.

Figure 2 One of the quickest ways to learn is to listen but it is easy to be distracted

Figure 3 The extra effort student B put into his notes will no doubt be worthwhile when he comes to revise

There are three different types of notes, each of which have their own advantages. You can choose which to use depending upon the type of information to be presented.

1. Structured notes

The information is presented in brief statements with lots of headings, subheadings and numbered points. There are no large sentences or paragraphs.

ENERGY

1. Types of energy

   a) light
   b) sound
   c) chemical
   d) electrical

When energy is changed work is done.

2. Sources of energy

   a) fossil fuels
   b) tidal
   c) wind
   d) solar

Fossil fuels are non-renewable sources of energy. They should be conserved if possible.

2. Spider diagrams

The main idea is placed in the centre and all other connected thoughts and ideas are added around it. These should be extremely brief, perhaps just one or two words. More detailed notes could be written on the opposite page. The spider diagram shows an overall view of connected ideas while the notes provide detail. Spider diagrams are very useful for planning essays or making brief notes when revising.

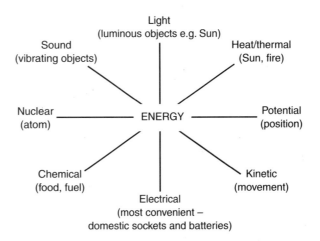

3. Pictures and diagrams

A picture is worth a thousand words. It is often a quick way of presenting, understanding and retrieving certain kinds of information. Here are a few different types of picture that you might find useful. Select those that best suit your needs.

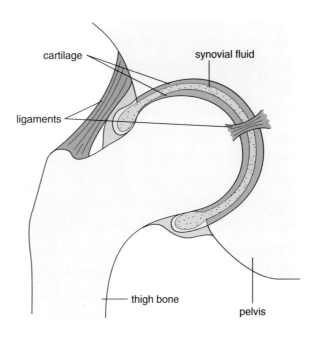

Figure 4 Diagrams like this give a good visual impression which reinforces text

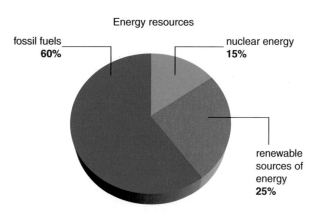

Figure 5 Pie charts are good for comparing several quantities at once

Planet	Time to orbit the Sun (years)
Mercury	0.2
Venus	0.6
Earth	1

Figure 6 Tables allow you to collect and record a lot of information in a very small space

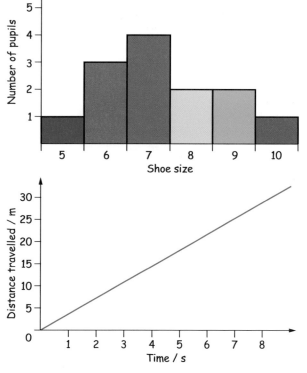

Figure 7 Graphs allow you to record a lot of information in a way which is very visual and compact. They enable you to make quick comparisons and see trends

4

Deciding where you are going to study?

A large amount of your studying is going to take place in school but there will also be times when you need to work at home. Finding the right place with the conditions that suit you is important. Here are some ideas you might like to consider.

Deciding where, when and how to revise

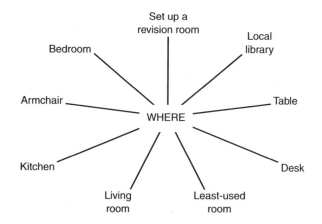

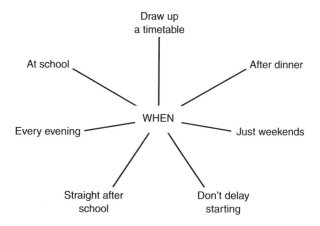

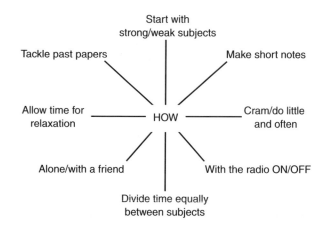

● EXAM REVISION

Towards the end of Year 9 you will take your National Tests in Science. A good revision programme and good revision techniques will help you to prepare.

1. Start early

2. Organise yourself

Collect together all the books you are going to need from Years 7, 8 and 9. Draw up a timetable for your revision like the one at the bottom of this page and stick to it.

Figure 8 By starting early you will go into your exams feeling confident and well-prepared. Don't follow the example of the student on the right who thought he could do all his revision the night before

Date	Topic 1	Topic 2	Topic 3
Monday 1 May	Make notes on different types of energy	Check Key Terms for types of energy	
Tuesday 2 May	Do questions at end of 'Energy' topic	Make notes on 'Energy Resources'	Check Key Terms for 'Energy Resources'
Wednesday 3 May	Do questions at end of 'Energy Resources' topic	Make notes on 'Using Energy'	Check Key Terms for 'Using Energy'
Thursday 4 May	Do questions at end of 'Using Energy' topic	Check out 'What you need to know' at end of section	
Friday 5 May	Do 'How much do you know?' questions at end of Energy section		

Guides to drawing up your revison timetable

1 Don't try to tackle too much in your revision slots. Try working for an hour, then reward yourself with a break of 15–30 minutes and then go back to your work for another hour.

2 Include 'time-out' sessions in your table. It is important that you don't become stale by working too hard and not relaxing. Keep a sensible balance between work and play.

3 Plan the order in which you want to tackle the topics. On days when you have lots of other things to do, such as homework or going out with your friends, choose an easy, straightforward topic. On days when you have a little more time, tackle more demanding areas.

4 Tick off the topics you have covered.

5 Try not to get behind with your revision once you have drawn up your timetable. You will revise much more efficiently if you know you are on top of things.

6 Make several copies of your timetable. Keep one copy in your school bag and stick one up in the kitchen or next to the TV set. This will mean that you won't miss a revision session and will enable your family to see how well your revision is going.

3. Tips on how to revise

a) As you read through your notes use a highlighter pen to mark key ideas and key words. The **Key terms** in this book have already been highlighted and listed for you.

b) Try to understand what you are reading. Don't try to memorise things parrot-fashion. The questions at the end of each topic give you the opportunity to make notes in your own words.

c) Write out key facts on separate cards. This will help to emphasise them.

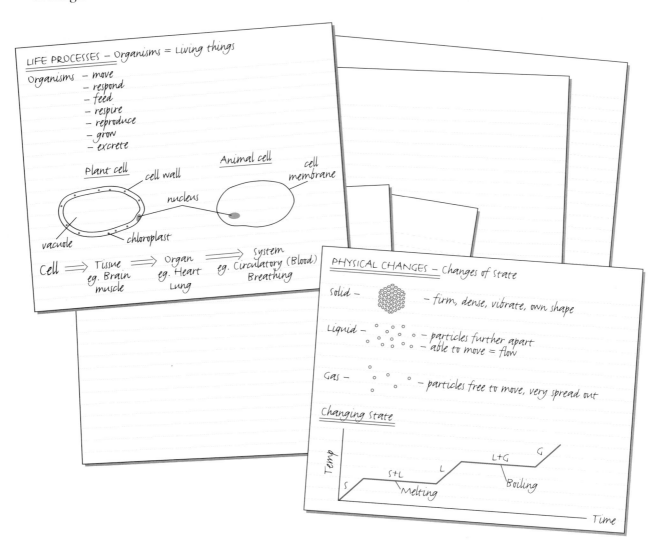

6

Figure 9 **Examples of some revision cards**

d) After you have read a piece of work (no more than one page at a time) try to explain to yourself what it is you have just learned or draw a spider diagram of the topic.

e) After you have finished a longer topic, perhaps 10 pages, go back over it glancing only at the highlighted headings and key terms. Check that you understand what they mean and why they are important. A summary of the key ideas, **What you need to know**, is given in this book at the end of each group of topics.

f) When you have finished several topics, try to tackle some questions from past papers. In this book you will find at the end of each group of topics examples of the different types of question you will meet in your exam.

Mnemonics and sayings

These can be useful memory joggers. Some examples are given here:

Red, **O**range, **Y**ellow, **G**reen, **B**lue, **I**ndigo, **V**iolet.

These are the colours of the rainbow in the correct order and can be remembered by the phrase

Richard **O**f **Y**ork **G**ave **B**attle **I**n **V**ain.

Many **V**ery **E**nergetic **M**en **J**og **S**lowly **U**pto **N**ewport **P**agnell.

This saying helps us to remember the names of the planets in order from the Sun – **M**ercury, **V**enus, **E**arth, **M**ars, **J**upiter, **S**aturn, **U**ranus, **N**eptune, **P**luto.

You could try making up some of your own, but keep them simple.

● THE DAY OF THE EXAM

1 Get up at your usual time and go through your normal routine. Your revision is complete, so be confident that you are well prepared. Concentrate on the idea that there are lots of topics you now understand really well. Don't become overworried if there are one or two topics you still haven't really grasped.

2 Make sure you have everything you need for the exam – pens, pencils, a rubber, a ruler, a protractor, a calculator and a spare ink cartridge.

3 Listen to the instructions you are given before the exam starts.

4 Fill in the front of your question sheet as instructed.

5 Try to answer all the questions. If you find one too hard, go on to the next question.

6 Keep an eye on the clock. Try to be about half way through the paper after half the exam time.

7 Follow the instructions given in the question. For example, if the question says 'Use a ruler to . . .' then you must use a ruler to gain full marks.

8 If the answer to a question is worth 3 marks, you will probably need to provide **three** pieces of information.
For example, if the question reads 'Which of the following planets are further from the Sun than the Earth: (A) Saturn, (B) Mercury, (C) Jupiter, (D) Venus, (E) Mars (3 marks)', you can assume that you will have to name three planets (correct answer, A, C and E).

9 Read your answers through when you have finished a question to make sure that you have written what you wanted to write and that you have answered the question asked.

10 Finally, try to write neatly. Everyone wants you to do well in your exams but if the examiner can't read your answer he can't give you the marks.

GOOD LUCK

● SCIENTIFIC INVESTIGATIONS

Many of your Science lessons will involve practical experiments. To do these accurately and safely requires skill. Your ability to cope with these experiments will be assessed by your Science teacher and the mark you are awarded will contribute to the final grade you obtain in your National Test in Science. Your Science teacher will make sure that you have lots of opportunities to practise these skills and you will be told when they are going to be tested.

There are four skill areas that will be tested.

1 Planning an experiment

In this area you will need to demonstrate that you can

◆ plan a simple experiment which is safe
◆ plan an experiment which is fair, in which you control everything that may affect your readings/observations
◆ select the right equipment for your experiment
◆ make a sensible prediction for your experiment, i.e. say what you think will happen and why.

2 Obtaining evidence

In this area you will need to demonstrate that you can

◆ use the apparatus safely and with skill
◆ take accurate readings and/or make accurate observations
◆ record your readings and observations clearly, accurately and in a suitable manner, for example in a table.

Figure 2 Obtaining reliable evidence safely

Figure 1 Planning a safe and fair test

3 Analysing the evidence and drawing conclusions

In this area you will need to demonstrate that you can

◆ construct diagrams, charts or graphs to help in the analysis of your evidence
◆ identify trends and patterns in your results
◆ draw conclusions from your results
◆ look back at your prediction and say whether or not it was correct
◆ link your conclusions with some scientific knowledge.

4 Evaluate your experiment and the evidence you have obtained

In this area you will need to demonstrate that you can

◆ recognise whether the evidence you have collected can be used to draw any firm conclusions
◆ recognise observations and measurements that do not fit a pattern and that may be faulty
◆ explain how and why faulty readings have occurred and suggest ways in which the experiment might be changed so that the evidence obtained is more accurate and/or more reliable.

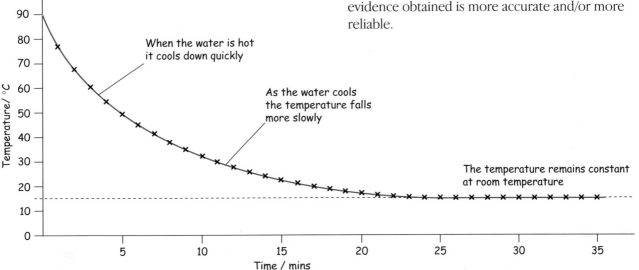

Figure 3 **Analysing your results**

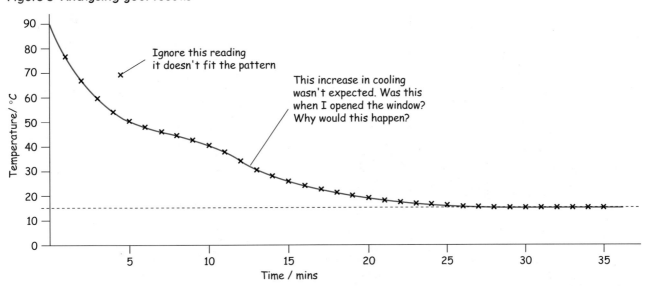

Figure 4 **Evaluating your results**

When you write up your experiment, make sure that there are no spelling mistakes and that your punctuation and grammar are accurate. There are marks available for these skills too!

LIFE PROCESSES & LIVING THINGS

1.1 LIFE PROCESSES

Are you alive?

Plants and animals are living **organisms**. You are a living organism. You are alive. There are seven characteristics which all living organisms show.

◆ All organisms **move**
◆ All organisms **respond to their surroundings**
◆ All organisms **feed**
◆ All organisms **release energy from their food**
◆ All organisms **reproduce**
◆ All organisms **grow**
◆ All organisms get rid of waste products they do not need i.e. they **excrete**.

Many non-living objects will show one or more of these characteristics of life but only 'living things' will show them all.

This list may help you to remember the characteristics of a living organism:

1 **O**btains food
2 **R**emoves waste
3 **G**rows
4 **A**dds to its own kind
5 **N**eeds energy
 Is
6 **S**ensitive to its surroundings
7 **M**oves

Figure 1 **This cartoon illustrates the characteristics of living organisms**

Cells

All organisms are made from simple building blocks called **cells**. The chemical reactions which are needed for living and growing take place inside these cells.

Plant cells

A typical plant cell has:

- a **nucleus** which controls the activities of the cell
- **cytoplasm** – a semi-liquid where most of the chemical reactions take place
- a **cell membrane** – a delicate skin which
  - holds the cell together
  - allows food and oxygen to enter the cell
  - allows waste products to leave the cell
- a **cell wall** made of cellulose which holds the plant cells together and gives them strength and support
- **chloroplasts** which absorb light energy so that the plant can make food
- a **vacuole** – a large central area containing **cell sap**, a watery liquid.

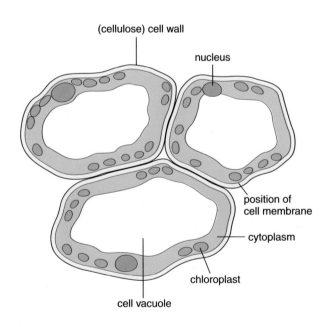

Figure 2 **Typical plant cells**

Animal cells

A typical animal cell has:

- a nucleus
- cytoplasm
- a cell membrane

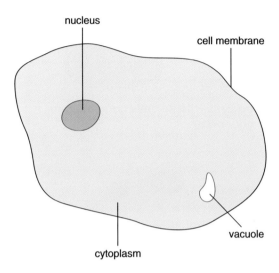

Figure 3 **A typical animal cell**

It has no chloroplasts and no cell wall; vacuoles are either very small or absent. The diagram given is of a simple organism called an amoeba. It has only one cell which has to do all the jobs – reproduce, move, feed etc.

Bigger and more complicated organisms like you and me are made from a variety of cells. Different cells carry out different jobs. There is a **division of labour**.

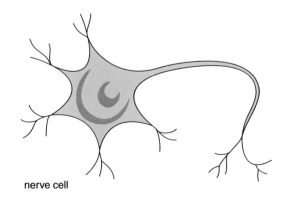

nerve cell

Figure 4 **Nerve cells – these cells carry messages around your body**

LIFE PROCESSES
continued

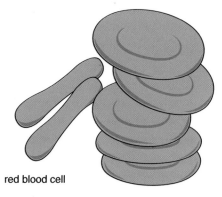

red blood cell

Red blood cells – these cells carry oxygen around your body

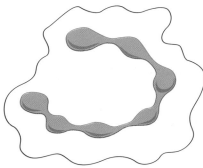

white blood cell

White blood cells – these cells kill germs that get into your body

sperm cell

Sperm cells – these cells are produced by the male. They are shaped like tadpoles so that they are able to swim

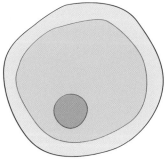

egg cell

12

Egg cells or ova – these cells are produced by the female. They are much larger than the sperm and are round like a ball

Key terms

Check that you understand and can explain the following terms:

- ★ organism
- ★ excrete
- ★ cell
- ★ nucleus
- ★ cytoplasm
- ★ cell membrane
- ★ cell wall

- ★ chloroplasts
- ★ vacuole
- ★ cell sap
- ★ division of labour
- ★ tissue
- ★ organ
- ★ system

Questions

1 Write down the seven features which all organisms share.

2 Draw a diagram of a) a plant cell, b) an animal cell.

3 Write down three differences between an animal cell and a plant cell.

4 Using the cells in your body as examples, explain the phrase *division of labour between cells*.

5 Explain the difference between a tissue and an organ. Give one example of each.

Groups of cells

Most plants and animals contain very large numbers of cells. Often cells will form groups in order to do a particular job. These groups are called **tissues**. Examples of tissues include skin tissue, blood tissue and muscle tissue. Tissues group together to form **organs** such as eyes, lungs, kidneys. Where several organs work together to perform an overall function they form a **system** such as the digestive system or the circulatory system.

What you need to know!

1 Most plants and animals have organs that enable life processes such as growth, reproduction and feeding to take place.

2 Plants and animals are made up of cells.

3 The function of cell membranes, cytoplasm and nuclei in plant and animal cells.

4 The function of chloroplasts and cell walls in plant cells.

5 Some cells have adapted and evolved so that they can carry out a particular task e.g. ova, sperm, nerve cells, root hair cells.

How much do you know?

1 Fish, birds, reptiles and human beings are all living things. Put a tick in four of the boxes below to show which four things all fish, birds, reptiles and human beings must do to stay alive.

Feed	Lay eggs	Breathe
Swim	Walk	Fly
Move	Excrete (get rid of waste)	Build nests

4 marks

2 This diagram shows the structure of a simple single-celled animal.

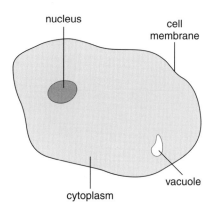

Explain what these parts of the animal cell do.

a) nucleus _____

b) cell membrane _____

2 marks

3 This diagram shows the structure of some typical plant cells.

(cellulose) cell wall

nucleus

position of cell membrane

cytoplasm

chloroplast

cell vacuole

Explain what these parts of the plant cell do.

a) chloroplasts _____

b) cell wall _____

2 marks

HUMANS AS ORGANISMS (1)

Food is vital for life. The kind of food you eat and the amount of food you eat affect your health and well-being.

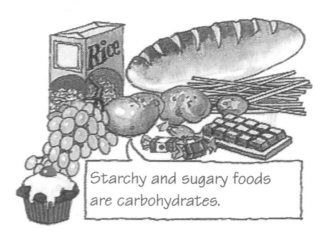

Figure 2 **Foods rich in carbohydrates**

Starchy and sugary foods are carbohydrates.

Figure 1 **Without the right kinds of food your body will suffer from malnutrition like the little boy in the photo above**

Fats are also energy-giving foods but they cannot release their energy quickly. It takes a long time for your body to use energy which is stored as fat. Butter, margarine, meat and fried foods contain lots of fats. Fats are very good insulators – your body uses them to prevent too much heat loss from your body. People who live in cold climates, like Eskimos, eat a diet rich in fat to keep them warm.

Healthy eating

There are five main types of food – **carbohydrates**, **fats**, **proteins**, **minerals** and **vitamins**. It is important that you eat these in the correct amounts. To be healthy you must have a **balanced diet**.

Carbohydrates are energy-giving foods. They can produce energy quickly. Bread, rice, pasta, flour, potatoes, chocolate and sugar all contain large amounts of carbohydrates. If you eat more carbohydrates than your body requires, they are stored as fat.

These foods contain fats and oils

14

Figure 3 **Foods rich in fats**

Proteins are body-building foods. They are used to help your body grow and repair any damaged tissue. Meat, cheese, eggs and nuts contain lots of protein.

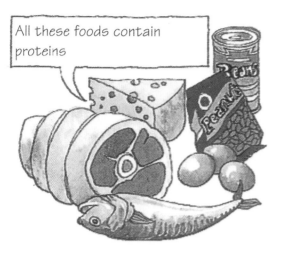

All these foods contain proteins

Figure 4 **Foods rich in protein**

Minerals are simple chemicals, found in most foods. Your body needs small amounts of them in order to work properly. For example, iron is needed in your blood so that it can carry oxygen to all parts of your body efficiently. Calcium and phosphorus are needed for strong, healthy bones and teeth.

Key terms

Check that you understand and can explain the following terms:

★ carbohydrates
★ fats
★ proteins
★ minerals
★ vitamins
★ balanced diet
★ water
★ fibre

Questions

1 Name five important types of food which you must have in your diet. Give two examples of the sources of each of these types of food.

2 Explain the phrase 'balanced diet'.

3 What will happen to you if you eat too many energy-giving foods?

4 Why is it important to eat food which contains fibre?

5 Find out the meanings of the words *malnutrition* and *obese*.

Figure 5 **Fish contains phosphorus and calcium. Milk contains calcium. Spinach contains iron. Meat contains phosphorus and iron**

Vitamins are complicated chemicals that must be present in the food you eat if the cells of your body are to work properly.

Fibre, vitamins and minerals are found in fruit and vegetables.

Figure 6 **A mixed diet of fresh foods will contain the various vitamins you need**

It is important that your diet also contains water and fibre.

Water is a vital ingredient in your diet. It is needed to transport many different materials around your body. Your body is almost three-quarters water!

Fibre helps to keep the digestive system clean and healthy. Brown bread, brown rice, fruit and vegetables contain lots of fibre. A lack of fibre can cause the lower part of the digestive system to become blocked. This is called constipation.

THE DIGESTIVE SYSTEM

You eat food to provide your body with substances it needs to live and grow. To be of any use this food has to be broken down into simpler substances, so it can dissolve in your blood stream and be carried to those parts of your body where it is needed. The breaking down of large food molecules into smaller molecules is called **digestion**.

Breaking down your food

Large food molecules, such as protein and starch, are broken down into smaller ones by chemical reactions. Special chemicals called **enzymes** help to speed up these reactions.

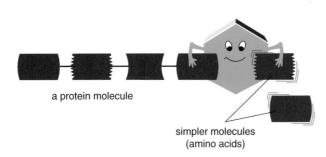

a protein molecule

simpler molecules
(amino acids)

Figure 1 **The enzyme pepsin helps to break proteins down into simpler molecules which can dissolve in blood**

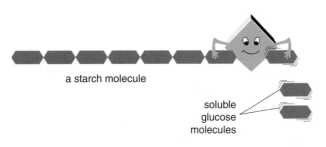

a starch molecule

soluble
glucose
molecules

Figure 2 **The enzyme amylase helps to break starch down into simpler molecules which are soluble in blood**

Passage of food through your gut

When you swallow your food it travels along a tube which begins at your mouth and finishes at your anus. This tube is called the alimentary canal or **gut**.

At various places along the gut **digestive juices** containing enzymes are produced. These react with the food, breaking it down as it passes through. This digested food is then able to pass through the wall of the gut into the blood. Food which has not been digested passes out of the anus.

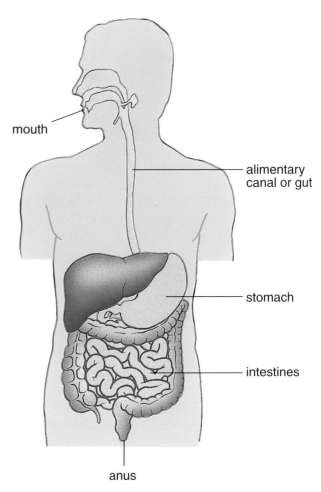

mouth

alimentary
canal or gut

stomach

intestines

anus

Figure 3 **The digestive system**

The stages of digestion

◆ Food is broken down mechanically by chewing.

◆ **Saliva** is produced by the salivary glands as you chew. This wets the food making it easier to swallow. Saliva contains an enzyme called amylase which begins the digestion of **starch** molecules.

◆ Food passes down the gullet to the stomach. No mechanical or chemical breakdown takes place while the food is in the gullet.

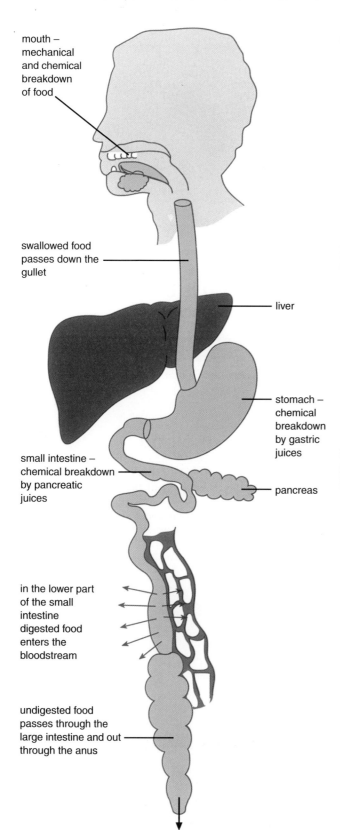

mouth –
mechanical
and chemical
breakdown
of food

swallowed food
passes down the
gullet

liver

stomach –
chemical
breakdown
by gastric
juices

small intestine –
chemical breakdown
by pancreatic
juices

pancreas

in the lower part
of the small
intestine
digested food
enters the
bloodstream

undigested food
passes through the
large intestine and out
through the anus

Figure 4 **The stages of digestion**

Key terms

Check that you understand and can explain the following terms:

★ digestion
★ enzymes
★ gut
★ digestive juices
★ saliva
★ starch
★ protein

Questions

1 What does your digestive system do for you?

2 What is an enzyme? Name two enzymes that are in your body.

3 Where does your gut begin and end?

4 Where in your body is food mechanically broken down?

5 Where in your body does digested food enter your bloodstream?

6 What happens to food which is undigested?

◆ When food enters the stomach more chemicals (gastric juices) are added to it. **Proteins** are digested by an enzyme called pepsin. Food stays in your stomach for about four or five hours. During this time, muscles in your stomach churn and mix the food with the gastric juices to help digestion.

◆ In the upper part of the small intestine, juices from the pancreas (pancreatic juices) which contain several enzymes are added. They continue to digest starches, proteins and fats. As the digested food travels along the small intestine (two to three hours) it passes through the thin walls and is absorbed by the blood.

◆ Undigested food passes through the large intestine and out of the body through the anus.

2.3 CIRCULATORY SYSTEM

Why do you need blood?

Your body contains about 5 litres of blood. Without it you could not survive.

Your blood

- carries heat to all parts of your body
- contains white blood cells which fight disease
- carries oxygen and digested food to the cells of your body
- carries carbon dioxide and other **waste products** away from these cells.

Blood is not a single substance. It is a mixture of

a) **red blood cells** – which pick up oxygen from the lungs and take it to the cells of your body where it is needed.

b) **white blood cells** – which help to protect you from disease.

c) **platelets** – blood cells which form clots to help stop the bleeding when you cut yourself.

d) **plasma** – a watery liquid which contains the cells detailed above together with several dissolved substances such as digested food (glucose), salts, hormones and waste products.

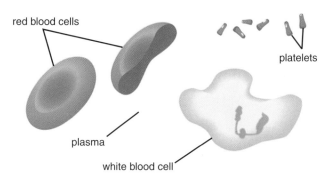

Figure 1 **The different components of blood**

How and why is blood moved around your body?

Every living cell in your body needs energy to survive. The ingredients necessary to produce this energy – glucose and oxygen – are carried to where they are needed by your blood (see Respiration page 24).

Circulation of blood

Blood is moved around your body by the pumping action of your heart. From your heart it is pumped to

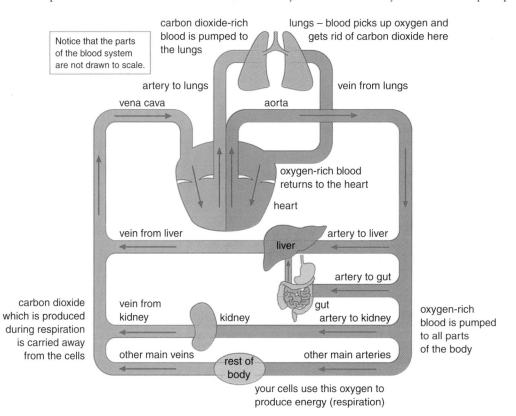

18

Figure 2 **The circulatory system**

your lungs where it picks up oxygen. This oxygen-rich blood then returns to the heart before being pumped to all parts of your body. Your cells use this oxygen to respire (produce energy). Carbon dioxide, which is produced during respiration, is carried away from the cells by the blood and returned to the lungs.

Blood vessels

Your heart pumps blood through a network of tubes called blood vessels. There are three different kinds of blood vessels.

1 **Arteries**. Blood which is rich in oxygen leaves your heart through tubes called arteries. These tubes are quite wide and have thickish walls as the blood is flowing under high pressure. When you feel your pulse, it is the pumping action of the blood through the arteries which you can feel.

2 **Veins**. Blood which is rich in carbon dioxide returns to the heart through tubes called veins. These tubes are often wider than arteries but have a thinner wall as the blood is under much less pressure. No pulse can be felt here as the blood flows smoothly through veins.

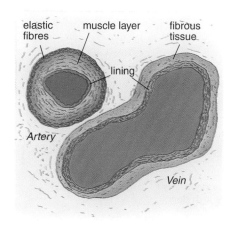

Figure 3 An artery and a vein

Key terms

Check that you understand and can explain the following terms:

★ waste product
★ red blood cell
★ white blood cell
★ platelet
★ plasma
★ artery
★ vein
★ capillary
★ diffuse

Questions

1 List four important jobs done by the blood in your body.

2 Blood is a mixture. Name four ingredients of this mixture and explain what each ingredient does.

3 Name three different types of blood vessel. Write a sentence about each type to explain the differences between them.

4 Draw a diagram to explain which substances are exchanged between the capillaries and the cells in your body.

5 Draw a spider diagram containing the key terms on these two pages.

3 **Capillaries**. As blood moves away from the heart it passes through narrower and narrower tubes until it eventually passes through a very fine network of tubes called capillaries. Every living cell in your body has a capillary close by so that glucose and oxygen can **diffuse** into the cell, and waste products, such as carbon dioxide, can diffuse out.

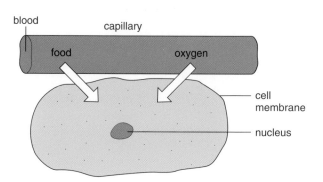

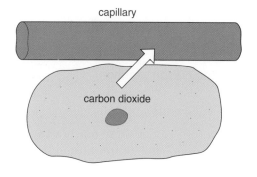

Figure 4 A capillary

HUMANS AS ORGANISMS (1)

The skeleton

Within your body there are 206 bones. These bones form your **skeleton**.

Your skeleton has several important functions:

◆ it supports your body, giving it shape.
◆ it protects your **vital organs**. For example, your heart and lungs are protected by the rib cage and your brain is protected by the cranium (skull).
◆ it is jointed in such a way as to allow movement.

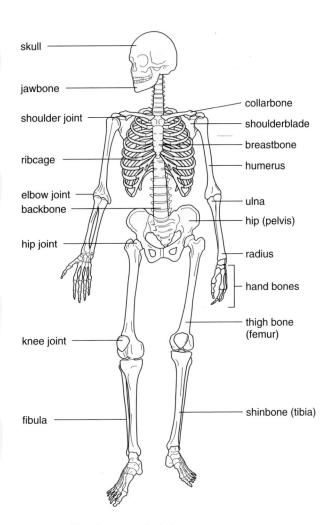

skull
jawbone
shoulder joint
ribcage
elbow joint
backbone
hip joint
knee joint
fibula

collarbone
shoulderblade
breastbone
humerus
ulna
hip (pelvis)
radius
hand bones
thigh bone (femur)
shinbone (tibia)

Figure 1 **The human skeleton**

Joints

You are able to move your arms and legs because they are attached to the rest of your skeleton by **joints**. There are two types of joint in your body which allow movement.

Hinge joints

Hinge joints allow a pivoting movement in just one plane. Your elbows and knees are hinge joints.

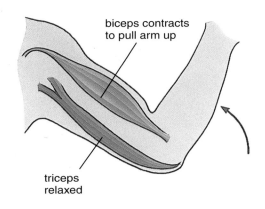

biceps contracts to pull arm up

triceps relaxed

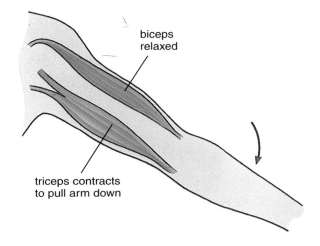

biceps relaxed

triceps contracts to pull arm down

Figure 2 **The elbow, a hinge joint**

In order to carry out all these functions your bones have to be strong enough to withstand knocks without breaking or bending. They must also be quite light so that movement is easy.

The two **muscles** which control the movement of your lower arm are called the biceps and the triceps. When you bend your arm upwards, the biceps contracts (shortens) and the triceps relaxes. When you straighten your arm, the biceps relaxes and the triceps contracts. This co-operative behaviour of muscles is the basis of movement. Pairs of muscles which behave like this are called **antagonistic pairs**.

Ball and socket joints

Ball and socket joints allow pivoting and rotational movement. Your shoulders and hips are ball and socket joints.

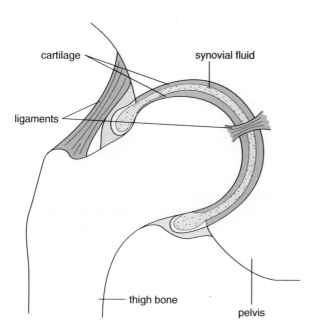

Figure 3 **The hip, a ball and socket joint**

Although these joints allow different degrees of movement, they do have certain features in common:

◆ the two bones forming the joint are held in place by fibrous tissue called **ligaments**. These limit your movements so that the bones don't move out of position, or dislocate.
◆ the bones are connected to the two muscles by a tissue called a **tendon**.
◆ in order to ensure that the bones can hinge and rotate smoothly, there is a lubricating liquid called **synovial fluid** within each joint.
◆ within the joint the bones are covered with a tough gristly material called **cartilage**. Like the synovial fluid, it encourages smooth movement between the bones of a joint.

Key terms

Check that you understand and can explain the following terms:

★ skeleton
★ vital organs
★ joints
★ hinge joints
★ muscles
★ antagonistic pairs

★ ball and socket joints
★ ligaments
★ tendons
★ synovial fluid
★ cartilage

Questions

1 What three important functions does a skeleton perform?

2 Why should bones be quite light but tough?

3 Name two different types of joint. In what way do these joints differ? List three ways in which these joints are similar.

4 The biceps and the triceps are a pair of antagonistic muscles. Explain what this statement means.

HUMANS AS ORGANISMS (1)

What you need to know!

1 A balanced diet contains carbohydrates, proteins, fats, minerals, vitamins, fibre and water.

2 Some sources of the different types of food needed in a balanced diet.

3 Food is needed to provide energy for your body.

4 Food is needed if your body is to grow and replace any damaged cells.

5 How digestion takes place in your body and how enzymes help this process take place.

6 Digested food is absorbed into your blood.

7 Waste products are passed out of your body.

8 How blood transfers important substances around your body.

9 How exchange of substances takes place at the capillaries.

10 How joints and muscles in your body allow you to move.

11 How antagonistic muscle pairs work.

How much do you know?

1 The diagram below shows a typical meal.

a) Which two parts of this meal are good sources of carbohydrates (energy providers)?

_____

2 marks

b) Which part of this meal is rich in protein – needed for growth and the repair of damaged cells?

_____

1 mark

c) Brown bread contains lots of fibre. Why is it important that we eat food that is rich in fibre?

_____

1 mark

2 Many people have unbalanced diets. This may cause illness or poor health.

Draw a line from each of the unbalanced diets on the left to the illness or health problem it may cause on the right.

not enough fibre   lacking energy

not enough calcium   heart disease

too much fat   weak teeth and bones

not enough protein   unable to get rid of undigested food (constipation)

not enough carbohydrate   poor growth

5 marks

3 The diagram below is of the human digestive system.

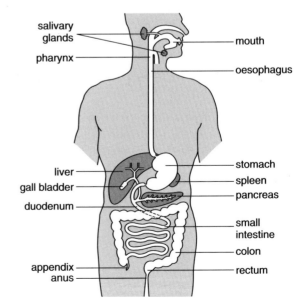

How much do you know? continued

a) Explain why starch and protein have to be digested before they can be absorbed into the bloodstream.

_____

1 mark

b) Where in your digestive system is food broken down mechanically?

_____

1 mark

c) Explain the function of enzymes in your digestive system.

_____

_____

1 mark

d) In which part of your digestive system does digested food pass into your bloodstream?

_____

1 mark

4 The table below shows three different kinds of blood vessel. Tick the box which correctly describes these vessels.

	Veins	Arteries	Capillaries
Very narrow tubes that allow substances to diffuse through their walls			
Tubes that carry oxygen-rich blood away from the heart			
Tubes that carry blood which has a lot of carbon dioxide dissolved in it			

3 marks

5 The diagram below shows an elbow joint.

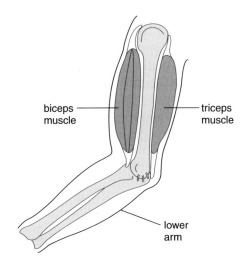

a) What happens to the biceps and triceps muscles when the lower arm is raised?

i) biceps

_____

ii) triceps

_____

2 marks

b) What happens to the biceps and triceps muscles when the lower arm is lowered?

i) biceps

_____

ii) triceps

_____

2 marks

HUMANS AS ORGANISMS (2)

All the living cells in your body need energy to survive. They usually obtain this energy from a chemical reaction between the food your body has digested (see page 16) and the oxygen from the air which you breathe. This process of obtaining energy is called **respiration**, the equation for which is given below.

glucose + oxygen → carbon + water +ENERGY dioxide

Figure 1 **Your body receives the energy it needs by respiration**

In everyday life, the rate at which your body needs oxygen for this reaction and the rate at which the blood supplies it are the same. An activity which keeps this balance, such as digging, is called an **aerobic exercise**.

In events of short duration, for example a 100 m sprint, your body will allow you to make greater demands on the supply of oxygen than it can cope with. At the end of the event you must repay this oxygen debt, usually by breathing rapidly, i.e. panting.

In longer events, such as marathon running or playing football, you may find that there is no opportunity to rest, so your oxygen debt grows. Your body helps you get over this problem by releasing the energy in your food using a different chemical reaction. This reaction does not need oxygen and is called **anaerobic respiration**.

glucose → lactic acid + ENERGY

Unfortunately one of the waste products of this reaction is a chemical called **lactic acid**. When lactic acid builds up in your muscles it makes them ache and may eventually cause cramp.

Breathing

How do you get air in and out of your lungs?

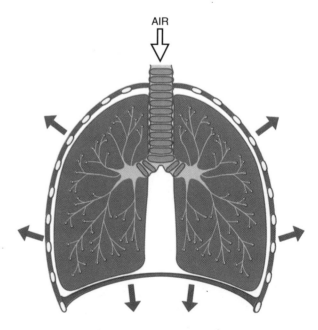

Figure 2 **When you breathe in, your rib cage moves upwards and outwards. A layer of muscle called the diaphragm moves downwards. These movements draw fresh air into your lungs**

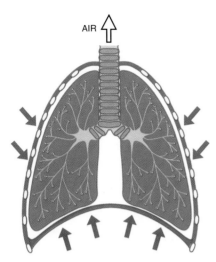

Figure 3 **When you breathe out, your rib cage moves down and inwards and your diaphragm moves up. These movements push the stale air out of your lungs**

The lungs

Once inside your lungs, the air you have breathed in travels through a network of fine tubes called **bronchioles** which lead to millions of tiny air sacs called **alveoli**. The alveoli are surrounded by a dense network of blood vessels (capillaries). Here oxygen can **diffuse** through the very thin walls of the alveoli into the blood. Carbon dioxide and water can diffuse in the opposite direction from the blood into the alveoli.

Key terms

Check that you understand and can explain the following terms:

- ★ respiration
- ★ glucose
- ★ aerobic exercise
- ★ anaerobic respiration
- ★ lactic acid
- ★ diaphragm
- ★ bronchioles
- ★ alveoli
- ★ diffuse

Questions

1 What is respiration?

2 Write down a word equation which explains what happens when aerobic respiration takes place.

3 Draw a labelled diagram to show how air is a) drawn into the lungs and b) expelled from the lungs.

4 Draw a labelled diagram to show how the gases move between an alveolus and a nearby capillary.

5 Why is smoking likely to make you feel out of breath when you run?

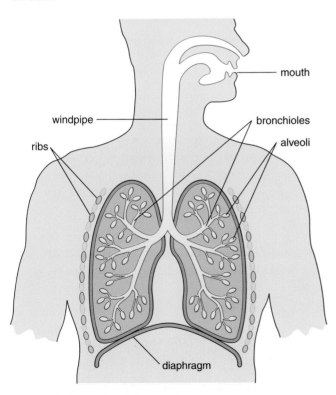

Figure 4 **The breathing system**

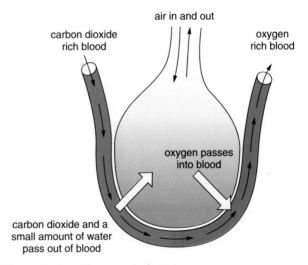

Figure 5 **Capillary and air sac**

The damage caused by smoking

The alveoli in your lungs are very delicate. If you smoke, you are likely to damage them. Less oxygen will then be able to diffuse into your bloodstream and you will feel breathless whenever you exert yourself.

Your body is an incredible 'human machine'. It has a highly advanced computer (your brain) controlling everything it does – breathing, digesting, moving. To keep your machine in good condition you must look after it.

Looking after your body

Regular exercise will strengthen the muscles of the heart and help to keep your body fit and healthy.

A **balanced diet** containing carbohydrate, protein, fat, minerals, vitamins and fibre will provide your body with all the materials it needs to grow fit and strong.

Figure 1 **A healthy human machine. By not smoking or drinking alcohol this athlete has avoided damaging his body. His stamina and general level of fitness will be high**

Abusing your body

If you mistreat or abuse your body you may damage it permanently.

Figure 2 **This man is seriously abusing his body**

Smoking can permanently damage your health. It affects the lungs and heart, causing illness and death.

A poor diet, e.g. eating too much of one kind of food, can lead to poor health because parts of your body are not receiving the substances they need to work properly. Imagine what would happen to a machine if no oil or grease was applied to its moving parts!

Too much fatty food can cause obesity and heart disease. Drinking too much alcohol can damage your liver.

Drugs

When taken under proper medical supervision, drugs can help people who are ill. When they are taken without medical supervision, they can seriously harm your body both mentally and physically. Ultimately, misuse of drugs can kill.

There are four main types of drugs:

1 **Painkillers**. These work by blocking out the messages of pain that go to the brain.
2 **Stimulants**. These also affect messages that go to the brain, causing it to work harder. This has the effect of making you feel more alert.
3 **Tranquillisers**. These work by slowing down the activity of the brain. They can cause drowsiness and affect a person's **reaction time** and **co-ordination**.
4 **Hallucinogens**. These cause people to feel, to see and to hear things that don't really exist.

The cost of drug abuse

Figure 3 **A drug addict damaging a machine that can never be replaced**

When the first effects of a drug wear off, people often feel depressed and weary. To overcome these feelings they feel the need to take the drug again. They may then become **addicted** to the drug – i.e. unable to live without it. If too much of a drug is taken – an **overdose** – it can cause permanent damage to the heart, liver and kidneys and may cause death.

Key terms

Check that you understand and can explain the following terms:

* regular exercise
* balanced diet
* painkillers
* stimulants
* tranquillisers
* reaction time
* co-ordination
* hallucinogens
* addicted
* overdose

Questions

1 Suggest three ways in which you can keep your body healthy.

2 Name the four main groups of drugs. Explain the effect each of these drugs would have on your body.

3 Why do drug takers often become addicted to drugs?

4 Name three ways in which drugs could damage your body.

Figure 4 **After the light-headed feelings pass, these young glue-sniffers will feel sick, suffer from acne around the face, possibly become unconscious and may even die**

Spreading germs

Your health can be affected by **germs**. These are very small organisms which can only be seen under a microscope. They can enter your body in several different ways:

◆ you may breathe in other people's germs which have been released into the air by their coughing or sneezing. The germs which cause cold and flu are spread like this.

◆ you may touch someone who is already infected. The germs which cause measles are spread in this way.

◆ you may be bitten by a bloodsucking insect, such as a mosquito, which puts germs into your bloodstream. Malaria is spread in this way.

◆ you may eat food which is contaminated with germs. Food poisoning is spread in this way.

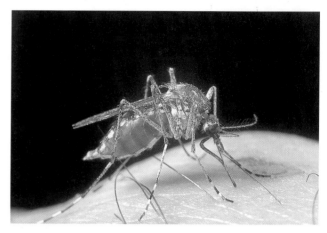

Figure 2 **Germs enter the bloodstream as the mosquito sucks blood out**

Why do I feel ill?

Once germs have entered your body they reproduce very rapidly. As they do so they feed on your body's cells, killing them. Some germs produce chemicals called **toxins** which are poisonous to your cells. You feel unwell because the germs are interfering with the workings of your body.

Figure 3 **Germs feed on your body's cells**

Most germs are either viruses or bacteria

Diseases caused by viruses	Diseases caused by bacteria
Measles	Whooping cough
Mumps	Pneumonia
Chickenpox	Typhoid
Polio	Blood poisoning

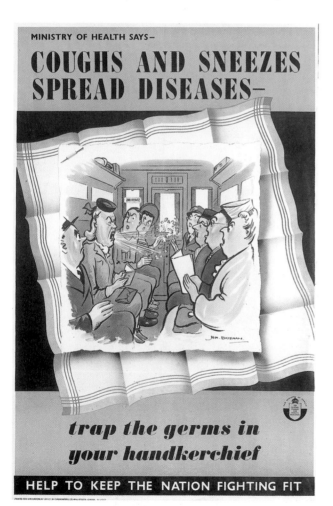

MINISTRY OF HEALTH SAYS—

COUGHS AND SNEEZES SPREAD DISEASES—

trap the germs in your handkerchief

HELP TO KEEP THE NATION FIGHTING FIT

Figure 1 **A World War II poster encouraging people to be aware of the dangers of germs**

Fighting illness

Your body has some **natural defences** to fight against invading germs. Your skin is the first barrier, however if germs do manage to get past this, your body has an **immune system** to deal with them. This is how it works.

Your blood contains several different types of white blood cells. These search out and kill anything which is not a normal part of your body. These cells:

- eat the invading germs
- make substances called **antibodies** which attack and kill germs
- react with the toxins to make them harmless.

Antibiotics and vaccination

Although your body is normally very good at dealing with invading germs, there are times when drugs and medicines can help. They help to speed up recovery from illness and act as reinforcements for your body's natural defences when the illness is life-threatening.

Antibiotics, such as penicillin, are medicines that will kill bacteria, but have no effect on viruses.

Vaccination prepares your immune system for invasion by a particular germ.

Figure 4

(a)

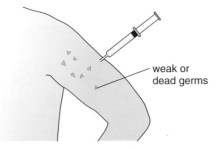

Weak or dead germs are injected into the bloodstream

(b)

The body produces white blood cells to fight the invading germs and any toxins they produce

Key terms

Check that you understand and can explain the following terms:

- ★ germs
- ★ toxins
- ★ natural defences
- ★ immune system
- ★ antibodies
- ★ antibiotics
- ★ vaccination
- ★ immunised

Questions

1 Name three ways in which germs can enter your body.

2 What is a toxin and how is it produced?

3 What are the two main groups of germs which invade your body? Name one illness caused by each type.

4 How does penicillin help your body to overcome certain illnesses?

5 How does your immune system react if germs invade your body?

(c)

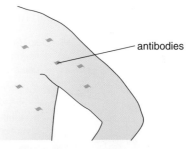

Even when all the germs have been killed, some of the antibodies remain in the blood ready to fight again if the same type of germ returns. Your body has been immunised against that disease

In Britain we vaccinate children against a variety of diseases:

- Diphtheria, Tetanus, Whooping cough and Polio at 6, 8 and 12 months
- Measles at 2 years
- Diphtheria, Tetanus and Polio at 5 years
- German measles (only girls) at 11–13 years
- Tuberculosis (TB) at 12–13 years.

29

REPRODUCTION

All human life begins by **sexual reproduction**. A baby starts its growth when a cell from its mother and a cell from its father join together to make a **fertilised egg**. The cell from the mother is called the **ovum**. The cell from the father is called the **sperm**.

Fertilising an ovum

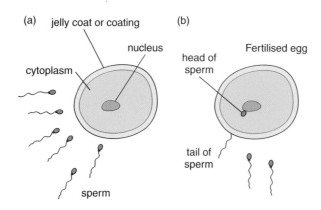

Figure 1 **Fertilisation**

Male and female reproductive systems

The differences between the male and female reproductive system can be seen in Figures 2 and 3.

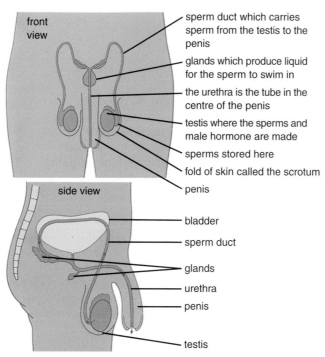

30

Figure 2 **The male reproductive system**

Sexual intercourse

When sexual intercourse takes place the **penis** of the man is inserted into the **vagina** of the woman. Sperm from the man's **testes** travel out of the penis, into the vagina, through the **womb** and into the **Fallopian tubes**. If there is an ovum in these tubes it may be fertilised.

Menstrual cycle or period

An ovum is released from a woman's **ovaries** about every 28 days. From the ovaries it travels down the Fallopian tubes. If the ovum is fertilised, it attaches itself to the wall of the womb where a lining has formed in readiness for the fertilised egg. If the egg is unfertilised, it and the lining pass out of the body through the vagina. This is commonly called having a **period**. The 28 day cycle of the release of an ovum, the development of the womb lining and the discharge of the lining out of the body if an egg is not fertilised is called the **menstrual cycle**.

Pregnancy

The human egg develops in the womb of the mother. For the first two months it is called an **embryo**. After two months it is called a **foetus** (pronounced 'feetus'). On average, **pregnancy** lasts

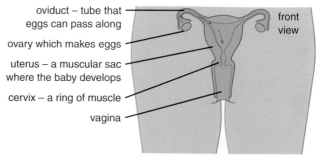

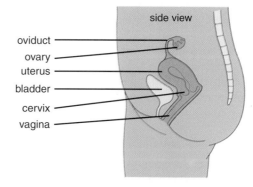

Figure 3 **The female reproductive system**

280 days or nine months. During pregnancy, the foetus receives all it requires to grow from its mother.

The foetus is connected by a tube called the **umbilical cord** to the **placenta**. In the placenta, food and oxygen from the mother's blood can enter the bloodstream of the foetus. The umbilical cord also transports waste from the baby's blood to the mother's.

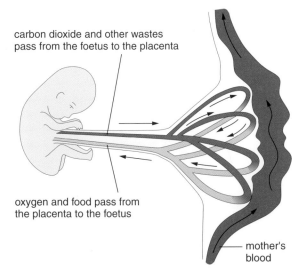

carbon dioxide and other wastes pass from the foetus to the placenta

oxygen and food pass from the placenta to the foetus

mother's blood

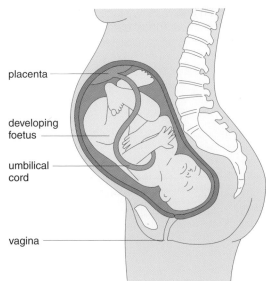

placenta

developing foetus

umbilical cord

vagina

Figure 4 **The development of the foetus during pregnancy**

Puberty and adolescence

Very young people cannot reproduce and make babies. It will be a few years before their reproductive organs begin to produce eggs and sperm. Once this starts to happen, other changes may also take place.

Key terms

Check that you understand and can explain the following terms:

* sexual reproduction
* fertilised egg
* ovum (ova)
* sperm
* penis
* vagina
* testes
* womb
* Fallopian tube
* ovaries
* period
* menstrual cycle
* embryo
* foetus
* pregnancy
* umbilical cord
* placenta
* puberty
* adolescence

Questions

1 Draw a labelled diagram of a) the female reproductive organs and b) the male reproductive organs.

2 Why do sperm have tails?

3 What is the maximum number of sperm that can fertilise one ovum?

4 On average how often is an ovum released from a woman's ovaries?

5 What is the function of the placenta?

6 What three physical changes may take place in a) boys and b) girls during adolescence?

◆ **Boys** (11–14 years old)
  – Their voices may break, i.e. become deeper.
  – They may begin to grow hair on their faces, chests and pubic regions and may become more muscular.
◆ **Girls** (10–14 years old)
  – Their breasts may enlarge.
  – They may grow hair around their pubic regions.
  – They may begin to have periods.

As well as all these physical changes, it is perfectly normal for boys and girls to experience some emotional changes, such as becoming more self-conscious and more aware of the opposite sex. This period of change from boyhood to manhood and from girl to woman is called **puberty** or **adolescence**.

What you need to know!

1 Physical and emotional changes take place during adolescence.

2 The main parts of the male and female reproductive system.

3 A human life begins when an ovum is fertilised by a sperm.

4 How a fertilised egg develops in the mother's womb and the important role the placenta plays in the embryo's growth.

5 The energy we need to live is released by respiration.

6 Aerobic respiration requires oxygen and food.

7 Oxygen + digested food (glucose) → carbon dioxide + water + ENERGY

8 How oxygen is drawn into the lungs.

9 How oxygen enters the bloodstream via the alveoli.

10 Carbon dioxide leaves the bloodstream and enters the lungs via the alveoli.

11 Smoking affects the structure of the lungs and makes the exchange of gases more difficult.

12 The abuse of alcohol, solvents such as glue, and other drugs can seriously affect your health.

13 Bacteria and viruses can cause illness.

14 Medicines and inoculation can help your body fight disease.

How much do you know?

1 The diagram below shows the female reproductive system.

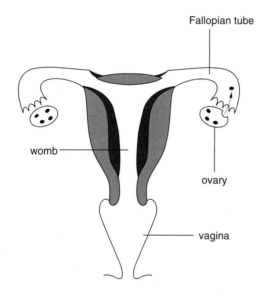

Fallopian tube

womb

ovary

vagina

a) Approximately how often is an ovum released from the ovaries?

☐ One every day
☐ One every 7 days
☐ One every 28 days
☐ One every year

1 mark

b) Where is an ovum normally fertilised by a sperm cell?

_____

1 mark

c) What happens to an ovum if it is not fertilised?

_____

1 mark

2 The diagram below shows a developing embryo attached by the umbilical cord to the placenta.

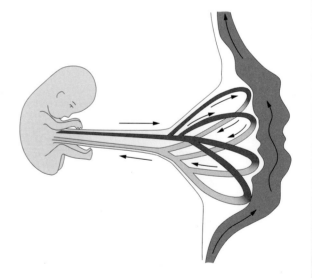

a) What two important substances pass from the mother through the placenta to the embryo?

_____

_____

2 marks

How much do you know? continued

b) Why should pregnant women not smoke?

_____

1 mark

3 What three changes may take place in boys or girls during puberty?

_____

_____

_____

3 marks

4 The diagram below is of an alveolus (air sac) and a capillary.

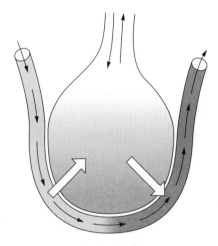

a) Which gas diffuses from the alveoli into the blood?

_____

1 mark

b) Which gas diffuses from the blood into the alveoli?

_____

1 mark

c) Explain why exercising makes a heavy smoker feel out of breath?

_____

_____

_____

2 marks

5 This is a diagram of a living cell.

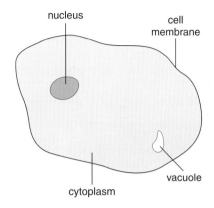

Which two substances does this cell need to be able to respire?

Tick the two correct boxes.

☐ salt
☐ water
☐ oxygen
☐ glucose
☐ carbon dioxide

2 marks

6 Your health can be affected by germs.

a) Name two illnesses that are caused by germs.

_____

_____

2 marks

b) Name two ways in which germs could enter your body.

_____

_____

2 marks

c) How does your body fight against these invading germs?

_____

_____

2 marks

d) Why is someone who has been vaccinated more able to fight against invading germs.

_____

_____

2 marks

3.1 PLANTS – MAKING FOOD

All plants and animals need food in order to live and grow. Animals obtain their energy from the food which they eat. Most plants make their own food from simple substances which are in the soil and the atmosphere by a process called **photosynthesis**.

Figure 1 **When photosynthesis takes place plants grow and make new** biomass

Photosynthesis

To make food by photosynthesis, plants need water from the soil, carbon dioxide from the air and light energy from the Sun.

◆ The water is drawn up through the **roots** and the **stem** to the leaves.
◆ The carbon dioxide enters the leaves through tiny holes or pores called **stomata**.
◆ The light energy is absorbed by a green substance called **chlorophyll** which is found in **chloroplasts** in the plant's cells.

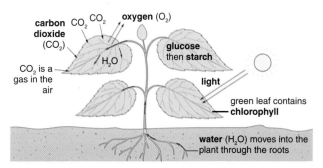

34

Figure 2 **Photosynthesis in a leaf**

The reaction which produces the plant's food is

$$\text{water} + \text{carbon dioxide} \xrightarrow{\text{sunlight}} \text{sugar (food)} + \text{oxygen}$$

The oxygen released by this reaction escapes into the atmosphere through the stomata. The sugar (sometimes called glucose) may be used by the plant straight away to produce the energy it needs to live (see Respiration) and to grow. Often the glucose is used to make more complicated substances such as

◆ **cellulose** – which is used to make plant cell walls
◆ **starch** – which is stored food that the plant can use later.

Respiration

Aerobic **respiration** is the process by which plants release the energy contained in food.

The reaction which produces this is the same as that for respiration in animals:

$$\text{oxygen} + \text{glucose} \rightarrow \text{carbon dioxide} + \text{water} + \text{ENERGY}$$

The oxygen needed for this reaction is taken from the atmosphere through the stomata.

The carbon dioxide produced is released through the leaves into the atmosphere

Day and Night

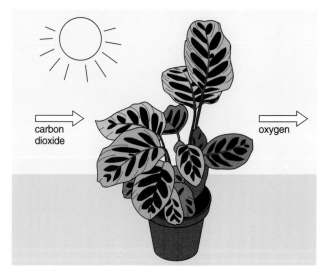

Figure 3 **During the daytime when there is light, photosynthesis takes place**

Figure 4 **During the night when there is no light, plants use some of their stored food for energy**

Plants make more oxygen during the daytime than they use at night. As a result they are continually supplying the atmosphere with oxygen. This oxygen is needed by all the animals which live on the Earth.

Transpiration

Plants lose a large amount of water from their leaves by evaporation. This loss of water is called **transpiration**.

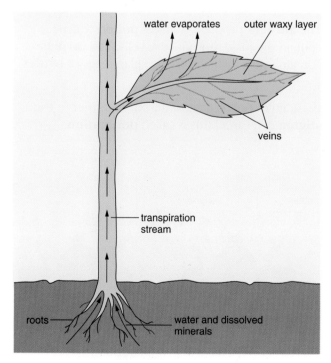

Figure 5 **Transpiration**

Questions

1 By what process do plants make their own food? Write down a word equation which explains how this food is made.

2 By what process do plants convert their food into the energy they need? Write down a word equation which explains how this happens.

3 Name two types of minerals a plant must absorb from the soil if it is to be healthy.

4 What are the tiny pores called through which carbon dioxide and oxygen enter and leave the leaves of a plant?

Transpiration occurs most rapidly in hot, dry, windy conditions. To prevent too much water from being lost in this way

◆ most plants have a waxy layer on their leaves.
◆ the size of the stomata on the surface of the leaves can be decreased.

The loss of water from the leaves draws new water and important minerals, such as nitrates and phosphates which are carried in the water, up from the roots through the stem. This upward flow of water through the stem is called the **transpiration stream**.

3.2 FLOWERING PLANTS

The structure of flowering plants

Plants have a structure which allows them to make and store the food they need to live, grow and reproduce. They have roots, a stem, and leaves. At certain times of the year they will also have buds and flowers.

Leaves

The leaves of a plant are the chemical factories where photosynthesis takes place, producing food.

They are often coated with a thin waxy layer on their upper surface to prevent them from losing too much water. This layer tends to be thicker for plants living in dry conditions. If a plant is losing water too quickly, it may reduce the size of the stomata on its leaves to help slow down the rate of evaporation.

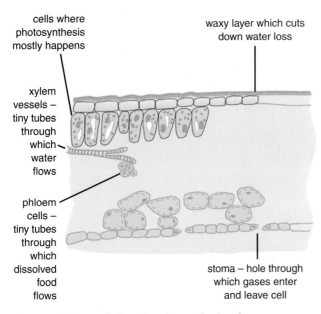

Figure 1 **The cellular structure of a leaf**

Stem

The stem is the main support for the plant. The cells here contain a lot of water which gives the stem 'stiffness'. If the plant is short of water, the stem loses this stiffness and the plant wilts.

Separate tubes carry water and food through the stem. **Xylem** tissue carries water. **Phloem** tissue carries food from the leaves where it is made to wherever it is needed.

Roots

The roots of a plant anchor it firmly in the ground. The root hairs on the surface of the root take in water and minerals from the soil. In some plants the roots are used to store energy e.g. turnips and carrots.

Sexual reproduction in plants

Plants have flowers so that they can reproduce. Most flowers contain both the male and female parts.

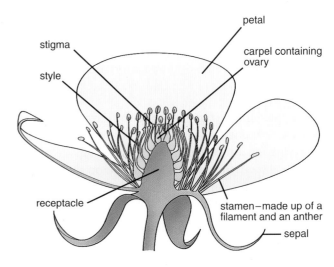

Figure 2 **The structure of a flower**

The **anthers** produce grains of **pollen** which contain the male reproductive cells. The **carpels** contain ovaries which produce plant eggs or **ovules**, the female reproductive cells.

If a grain of pollen is moved from an anther to the **stigma** of a carpel this is called **pollination**.

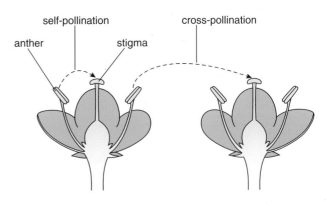

Figure 3 **Pollination**

If the pollen has been moved by the wind, the plant has been **wind-pollinated**. If the pollen has been moved by insects, the plant has been **insect-pollinated**.

When a grain of pollen sticks to the carpel, a tube grows down through the ovary. The nucleus of the pollen then travels along this tube and fertilises an ovule. The fertilised ovule grows to form a **seed** from which a new plant can be grown. The ovary of a flower often grows into a **fruit** which protects the developing seeds.

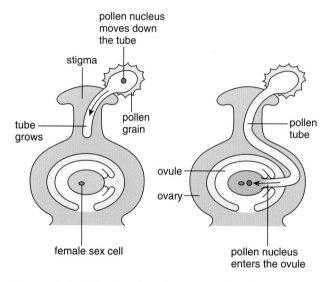

Figure 4 **Fertilisation in a flowering plant**

Spreading the seeds

To ensure that seeds have a good chance of survival they need to be scattered over as large an area as possible. This is called **seed dispersal**.

Key terms

Check that you understand and can explain the following terms:

* xylem
* phloem
* anther
* pollen
* carpel
* ovule
* stigma
* pollination
* wind-pollination
* insect-pollination
* seed
* fruit
* seed dispersal

Questions

1. What causes a plant to wilt?
2. Which part of a plant anchors it into the ground?
3. What is the name of the male part of a flower and what does it produce?
4. What is the name of the female part of a flower and what does it produce?
5. Explain the difference between pollination and fertilisation.
6. Explain one way by which the seeds of a plant can be spread.

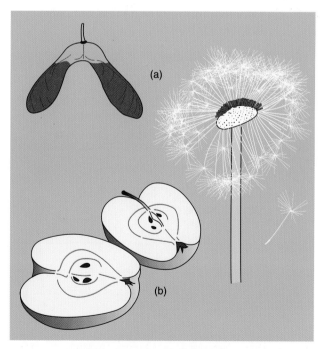

Figure 5 a) **These seeds are shaped so that they are easily dispersed by the wind** b) **These seeds are surrounded by tasty fruit and are spread by the animals that eat them**

What you need to know!

1 Photosynthesis produces food for plants and oxygen as a waste product.

2 Plants need carbon dioxide, water and light for photosynthesis to take place.

3 Water + carbon dioxide $\xrightarrow{\text{sunlight}}$ sugar (food) + oxygen

4 Plants need oxygen to respire.

5 Plants need small amounts of elements such as nitrogen and phosphorus.

6 Root hairs absorb water and minerals from the soil.

7 How sexual reproduction takes place in flowering plants.

8 How fertilisation occurs and seeds develop.

How much do you know?

1 The diagram below shows a flower which has been cut in half. A, B and C are different parts of the flower.

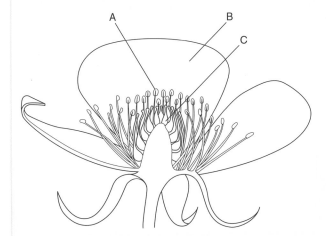

a) Put the correct letter next to the part of the flower in this table.

Part of flower	Letter
anther	
carpel	
petal	

3 marks

b) What is the job of part B?

_____

_____

1 mark

c) What is the job of part C?

_____

_____

1 mark

2 The diagram below shows an insect visiting a flower in search of food.

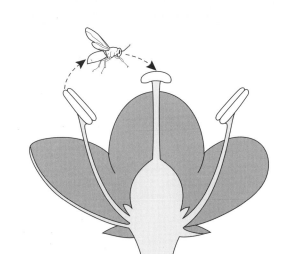

a) Whilst the insect is feeding, some pollen from the _____ is transferred to the stigma. This process is called _____ .

2 marks

b) Suggest a second way in which the pollen could be moved.

_____

_____

1 mark

c) Which part of the flower contains the male cells?

_____

1 mark

d) Which part of the flower contains the female cells?

_____

1 mark

How much do you know? continued

3 The diagram below shows a strawberry plant. A, B, C and D are different parts of the plant.

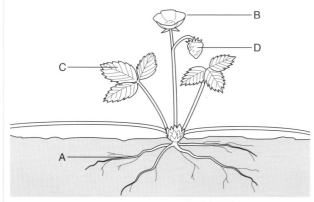

a) Put the correct letter next to the part of the plant in this table.

Part of plant	Letter
flower	
root	
leaf	
fruit	

4 marks

b) Which part of the plant

   i) produces the food the plant needs?

_____

1 mark

   ii) protects the seeds?

_____

1 mark

   iii) draws water and minerals from the soil into the plant?

_____

1 mark

   iv) attracts insects to the plant?

_____

1 mark

4 a) Write down a word equation which describes how a plant produces food.

_____

5 marks

b) When campers take their tents down after a fortnight's holiday in the summer, they notice that the grass where the tent has been is yellow. Explain why this happens.

_____

_____

3 marks

c) What happens to the grass after the tent has been removed?

_____

2 marks

d) What would happen to the grass if the tent was left in the same place for the whole of the summer?

_____

1 mark

5 a) Write down the word equation which describes how a plant obtains its energy from food.

_____

4 marks

b) What is this process called?

_____

1 mark

c) What happens to food which is not immediately used to produce energy for a plant?

_____

1 mark

6 a) Name two gases that enter or leave the leaf through the stomata.

_____

_____

2 marks

b) Name one liquid which escapes through the stomata.

_____

1 mark

Variation

There are often large differences between animals of different **species**.

Figure 1 **The variety of life**

Even within a single species there can be differences. These differences are called **variations**.

Figure 2 **These kittens are from the same litter but already there are variations in colour, size and personality**

There are two types of variation – **continuous variation** and **discontinuous variation**.

Continuous variations

Your height, weight and foot size are examples of continuous variations. They are influenced by

◆ the circumstances and conditions of your upbringing
◆ **characteristics** you have **inherited** from your parents.

Figure 3 **The heights of each of these pupils will depend upon their diet and the genes they have inherited from their parents**

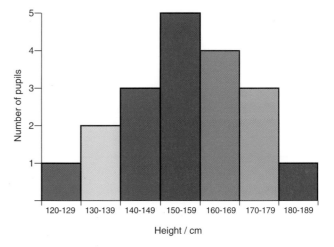

Figure 4 **A graph to show continuous variation in pupil height**

Discontinuous variations

Your blood group, eye colour and hair colour are examples of discontinuous variations. They are only influenced by the **genes** you inherited from your parents. These variations have no in-between values.

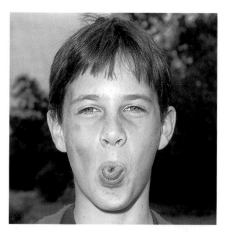

Figure 5 **Either you can do this with your tongue or you can't. It is something you have or have not inherited from your parents**

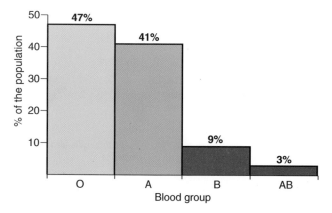

Figure 6 **A graph to show discontinuous variation**

Selective breeding

Selective breeding takes advantage of variations. It is used to try to breed plants and animals with a particular characteristic, for example a cow which gives more milk, a sheep that produces more wool or a plant which is resistant to disease.

Figure 7 **A thoroughbred racehorse**

Questions

1 Give three examples of
   a) continuous variations
   b) discontinuous variations.

2 What two characteristics would you want to breed into
   a) sheep which are grown for both their wool and their meat
   b) wheat which is grown in a hot, dry country
   c) a blackberry plant?

3 Make a note of the eye colour of all the pupils in your class. Now draw a graph of the colour of the eyes against the number of pupils who have that colour.

To produce this magnificent animal, the horse breeder has chosen to mate a stallion and a mare that have some of the features which he considered important for a horse to run quickly. He may, for example, have chosen a mare with long legs and a stallion with strong leg muscles. The first offspring of this mating may or may not have the desired features – it is a matter of luck. Eventually, however, it is likely that one of the offspring will inherit both the desired characteristics. He may then have a winner!

Plants can also undergo selective breeding. It is possible to **cross pollinate** beautiful red roses with strongly scented roses to produce a rose with both characteristics.

41

VARIATION, CLASSIFICATION AND INHERITANCE

VARIATION, CLASSIFICATION AND INHERITANCE

Figure 1

Trying to find a tin of soup or a piece of cheese in this supermarket is really easy. Similar items such as fish, meats or cheeses have all been gathered together into groups. These groups are then sorted into even smaller groups containing the different types of fish, meats or cheeses.

Let's suppose you want to find a tin of soup. You will probably use the signs and labels to do the following:

◆ enter the food hall
◆ find the shelves with the tinned food
◆ find the shelf with the soups
◆ find the part of the shelf which has the flavour of soup you want.

It's easy. But it would be a nightmare if the items in the store were not arranged in groups! This sorting into groups is called **classifying**.

Classifying organisms

There are over 1 million different things that live on the Earth. In order to study them more easily, scientists have classified them.

The five largest groups of living things are called **kingdoms**. These kingdoms are then sorted into smaller and smaller groups just like the items in the supermarket. A small part of the classification of the animal kingdom is shown below.

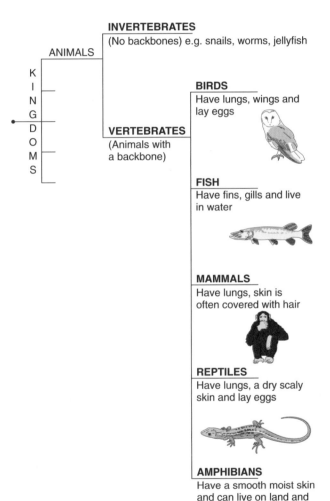

Figure 2 **A simple classification of the animal kingdom**

Keys

If you want to identify a plant or an animal you can do so using a **key**. Try this beetle key. Can you identify the names of each of the beetles?

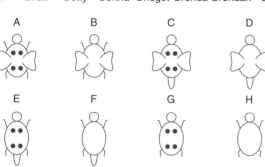

Does it have spots?

Yes — No

Does it have wings? — Does it have wings?

Yes — No — Yes — No

Does it have a tail? — Does it have a tail? — Does it have a tail? — Does it have a tail?

Yes No — Yes No — Yes No — Yes No

Bill — Brian — Betty — Bertha — Bridget — Brenda — Brendan — Bob

A   B   C   D

E   F   G   H

Figure 3 A beetle key

See if you can identify the tree from which each of these leaves came using the key given underneath.

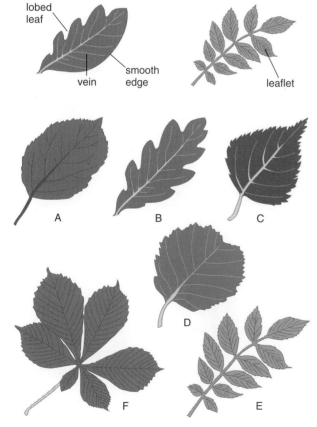

lobed leaf

vein   smooth edge

leaflet

A   B   C

D

F   E

Figure 4 A leaf key

Key terms

Check that you understand and can explain the following terms:

★ classification ★ bird
★ kingdom ★ fish
★ vertebrate ★ reptile
★ invertebrate ★ amphibian
★ mammal ★ key

Questions

1 Explain, in as much detail as you can, how the books in a library are classified.

2 What is a vertebrate? Give one example of a vertebrate.

3 What is an invertebrate? Give one example of an invertebrate.

4 What are the main differences between a reptile and an amphibian? Give one example of each.

5 Choose any eight books then make up a key to identify each of them.

1. Is the leaf simple (no leaflets)? Y ....GO TO 2
                                     N............GO TO 5

2. Is the leaf lobed?   Y ....GO TO 3
                                     N............GO TO 4

3. Do the veins spread out from
    a single point?   Y ....MAPLE
                                     N............OAK

4. Is the leaf triangular?   Y ....BIRCH
                                     N............ALDER

5. Are the leaflets in pairs?   Y ....ASH
                                     N............HORSE
                                          CHESTNUT

43

What you need to know!

1 There is variation within species and between species.

2 Variation within a species can be caused by both the environment and the characteristics inherited from parents.

3 Selective breeding can be used to produce new, improved varieties.

4 Living things are classified into groups, for example kingdoms.

5 Keys can be used to identify plants and animals.

How much do you know?

1 The diagrams below show different types of animals.

The animals can be put into four groups. The table below describes the main characteristics of each group.

Group A	Birds	Wings, feathers, two legs and a beak
Group B	Mammals	Body hair
Group C	Reptiles	Dry scales
Group D	Fish	Fins, gills and wet scales

Using the information in the table decide to which group each belongs.

Animal Number 1   Group_____
Animal Number 2   Group_____
Animal Number 3   Group_____
Animal Number 4   Group_____

4 marks

2 The diagram below shows one way in which living things can be classified.

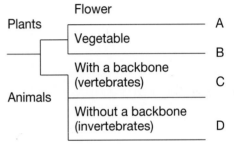

To which group, A, B, C or D, do each of the following living things belong?

dandelion   _____
lion   _____
jellyfish   _____
carrot   _____
tulip   _____
monkey   _____
worm   _____
human   _____

7 marks

3 The graph below shows the percentage of people who have a particular blood type. i.e. xx% of people have type y blood.

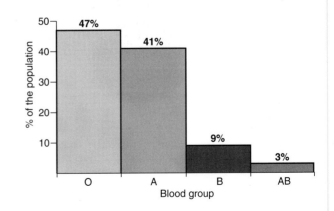

How much do you know? continued

a)   What kind of variation is this?

_____

1 mark

b)   'This kind of variation is **inherited** from parents'.
     Explain what this sentence means.

_____

1 mark

c)   A dog breeder wants to breed a dog which has
     no spots. Which two dogs shown below should
     he choose?

A

B

C

1

2

3

_____ and _____

2 marks

Habitats and adaptation

A **habitat** is a place where plants and animals live. The conditions of a habitat are called its **environment**. The environment, for example temperature, amount of light, oxygen and moisture, determines which animals and plants can live in that habitat.

Figure 1 **This habitat has the right conditions for trees, birds and woodland animals to live and grow**

Figure 2 **A cold habitat**

The habitat of this polar bear is very different to the woodland habitat. In order to survive here the polar bear has had to **adapt** to the extreme cold.

To survive here polar bears must

a) have a very thick fur coat to help keep them warm
b) have layers of fat beneath their fur. Fat is an excellent insulator and so prevents too much heat loss
c) **hibernate** during the winter when the conditions become too severe.

Figure 3 **A hot, dry habitat**

The habitat for camels and desert plants is an extremely hot and dry one.

Camels are able to survive here because they

a) can store fat in their humps
b) have large feet so that they can walk over the desert sand without sinking into it
c) have long eye lashes which help to stop sand being blown into their eyes.

For plants to survive here it is important that they do not lose too much water by evaporation from their leaves. In cacti, the leaves have been reduced in size to spines and water is stored in the centre of the plant from where there is little evaporation.

Changing conditions

The conditions in a habitat are constantly changing, both daily with the rising and setting of the Sun, and seasonally. These changes affect the plants and animals that live there.

Day and night

The word daisy comes from Latin and means 'eye of the day'. Like many other flowers, the petals of a daisy open out during the day when there is lots of light but close up again at night.

Figure 4 **Daisies during the day and during the night**

Most animals will hunt, eat and move around their habitat in the daytime. At night they hide away and sleep. **Nocturnal** animals, such as owls, bats and badgers, react differently to these changes. They are more active at night and sleep during the day.

Figure 5 **Animals like this owl have adapted to hunting in the dark. They have very keen hearing and eyesight. They fly almost silently**

Questions

1 What is a habitat? Give one example of a habitat.

2 What conditions might affect the plants and animals that live in a particular habitat?

3 Give one example of an animal which has adapted to a) a cold habitat and b) a hot habitat.

4 Name two animals that are nocturnal. How have these animals adapted to these conditions?

5 Name four ways in which plants or animals alter their behaviour to suit the changes in their environment when winter approaches.

Seasonal changes

As the seasons change, the temperature and length of day alter. Plants and animals adapt their behaviour to suit these changing conditions. For example in winter

◆ birds like swallows **migrate**. They fly to warmer countries.
◆ many trees lose their leaves and stop growing to save energy.
◆ some animals grow thicker coats and then get rid of them when summer approaches.
◆ some animals like hedgehogs hibernate.
◆ some plants like daffodils lie **dormant** below the ground as bulbs or seeds until the conditions become warmer.

47

5.2 FOOD CHAINS AND WEBS

Food chains

All plants are **producers** because they make their own food (see Photosynthesis, page 34).

Grazing animals, such as cows and sheep, are examples of **consumers** because they obtain the energy they need to live by eating plants such as grass. Because they eat the producers directly, they are called **primary consumers**.

Human beings eat the meat of cows and sheep. We are **secondary consumers**.

bird of
prey –
**tertiary
consumer**

shrew –
**secondary
consumer**

earthworm –
**primary
consumer**

leaf of an
oak tree –
producer

Figure 1 **This is an example of a** food chain

Here are some more examples of food chains:

weeds → tadpole → fish
grass → rabbit → fox
leaves → caterpillars → bluetits → kestrel
grass → insects → hedgehog
wheat → mouse → owl
weeds → minnows → trout → man

48 In each case energy is passed along the chain from the producers to the consumers.

Animals which only eat plants are called **herbivores** e.g. rabbits.

Animals which only eat meat are called **carnivores** e.g. tigers (see page 51).

Animals which eat both plants and animals are called **omnivores** e.g. man.

Food pyramids

Food chains, like those given previously, can also be drawn as **food pyramids**. These show how a large number of producers are needed to support bigger and fewer consumers.

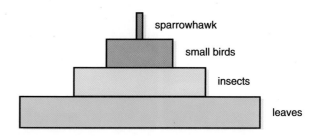

Figure 2 **An example of a** food pyramid

Food webs

Plants and animals rarely belong to just one chain. Several connected food chains are called a **food web**.

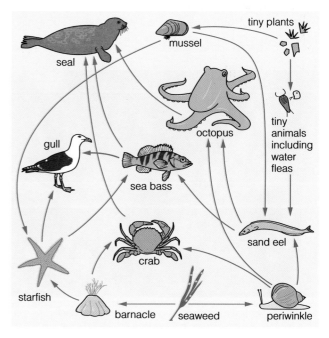

Figure 3 **A food web**

Poisons in food chains and food webs

Farmers often spray their crops with chemicals to increase their harvest or protect them from insects and disease. At the beginning of a food chain the concentration of these chemicals is quite low, but higher up the food chain the concentration of the chemicals increases and may be high enough to kill.

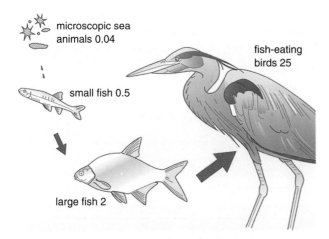

sea water 0.000003

microscopic sea animals 0.04

small fish 0.5

large fish 2

fish-eating birds 25

Figure 4 **The numbers compare the concentration of a chemical in different levels of a food chain**

wheat → mouse → owl

In this food chain it is the owl which is in greatest danger of being poisoned. The mouse eats many ears of wheat. The owl eats lots of mice. So the owl will consume the most poison.

Key terms

Check that you understand and can explain the following terms:

- ★ producer
- ★ consumer
- ★ primary consumer
- ★ secondary consumer
- ★ food chain
- ★ herbivore
- ★ carnivore
- ★ omnivore
- ★ food pyramid
- ★ food web

Questions

1 What is a producer? Give two examples of producers.

2 What is a consumer? Give two examples of consumers.

3 Give one example of a food chain which contains at least two consumers.

4 Give one example of a food pyramid. What do food pyramids show?

5 What is a food web? Why are animals at the end of food chains and webs most likely to die from any poison which is present lower down the chain?

5.3 COMPETITION AND SURVIVAL

Limited resources

All habitats have limited amounts of water, food, light and places to live. Plants and animals must **compete** with each other for these **resources**. Some have adapted so that their needs are different from their neighbours. Some have adapted so that they can compete more successfully. Competition leads to the **survival of the fittest**.

Trees in the South American rainforests (Figure 1) compete with each other for the sunlight which they need to survive. This is the main reason why they grow so tall. At the very top of the trees where there is bright sunlight there is a thick canopy of leaves. On the floor of the forest only plants and shrubs which can survive with very little light can grow.

Figure 1 **The South American rainforest**

Plants may compete for light, space, water and insects for pollination. Figure 2 shows how plants have adapted to out-compete other plants in the same habitat.

- The plants are of different heights – plants that are tall will receive most light. Only small plants that require little light will survive between the larger ones.
- The plants have roots of different lengths – grasses and dandelions survive next to each other on lawns because their roots take water from different depths of soil.
- The plants have flowers – one plant with few but large flowers, a second with a lot of little flowers.
- To attract insects to their flowers, plants may have strongly scented flowers, large colourful flowers or very large numbers of flowers.

Animals may compete for food, water, space or territory, and mating partners.

Figure 3 **Competition between animals**

Figure 2 **Competition between plants**

Many animals avoid these kinds of problems by establishing a territory. Robins sing loudly to warn other robins that the territory is occupied and defend it against intruders, particularly at breeding time.

Life and death

Figure 4 **A magnificent predator**

Living in the same habitat as this tiger could be hazardous. It is a **predator**. It hunts **prey**. Tigers have had to adapt in order to become successful predators:

◆ they are well **camouflaged**. Their striped coats help them to stalk their prey whilst hidden in forests and long grasses.
◆ they have developed very strong, powerful muscles so that they can run quickly and pounce on their prey.
◆ they have long claws and sharp teeth to grip and eat their prey.

Catch me if you can

Questions

1 What resources might a) plants and b) animals compete for?

2 Explain how two plants such as grasses and dandelions have adapted so that they can avoid competing for water.

3 Give three examples of animals that are predators. For each predator give one example of its prey.

4 Explain the phrase *natural selection* or *survival of the fittest*.

Passing on the 'trick'

Plants and animals that have an adaptation or a 'trick' which helps them survive will pass this on to many of their offspring. Those without the trick are less likely to survive. Eventually this trick becomes a natural feature for that organism. This is called **natural selection** or survival of the fittest.

Figure 5 **Adaptations to avoid predators: hares have good hearing, sharp eyes and run fast; bees and wasps have stings and warning colours; hedgehogs have spines; and fish swim in big groups**

What you need to know!

1 Different habitats support different plants and animals.

2 Plants and animals have adapted to respond to daily and seasonal changes that take place in their habitat.

3 Feeding relationships – food chains, food pyramids and food webs.

4 Toxic materials can build up in food chains.

5 What factors affect the size of populations e.g. predators, competition for food, water and light.

6 Plants and animals that compete for resources successfully can pass these qualities on to the next generation.

How much do you know?

1 A group of pupils studied the living organisms in a wood for several months. They made the following observations.

◆ Weasels eat wood mice
◆ Blue tits and great tits eat caterpillars
◆ Sparrowhawks eat blue tits and great tits
◆ Caterpillars eat oak leaves
◆ Wood mice eat acorns from oak trees
◆ Aphids eat oak leaves
◆ Blue tits and great tits eat aphids

Use this information to complete these food chains.

a) Oak leaves → _____ → _____

2 marks

b) Acorns → _____ → _____

2 marks

c) What is the producer for both of these chains?

_____

1 mark

d) From the observations name one consumer.

_____

1 mark

2 The food web below shows the feeding relationships between several organisms.

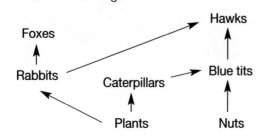

a) From the food web name one herbivore.

_____

1 mark

b) From the food web name one omnivore.

_____

1 mark

c) If the number of rabbits decreases:

i) How will this affect the number of foxes?

_____

1 mark

ii) How will this in turn affect the number of plants?

_____

1 mark

3 This is a food chain for organisms that live in a pond.

plants → slugs → toads

The graph below shows how the numbers of these organisms change over a period of time.

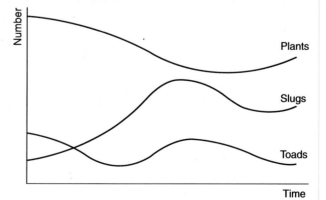

How much do you know? continued

a) What happens to the slug population as the number of toads reaches its maximum?

_____

1 mark

b) What is happening to the plant population during this time?

_____

1 mark

c) Explain why the plant population is changing in this way.

_____

_____

1 mark

Pike are predators. They eat toads.

d) Explain what would happen to the slug population if a pike was put into this small pond.

_____

_____

_____

2 marks

4 The diagram below shows four different birds that have successfully adapted to their habitats.

curlew

swift

owl

woodpecker

Write down the name of the bird which has adapted so that it can:

a) catch and eat mice

_____

1 mark

b) hunt for food deep in sand

_____

1 mark

c) hunt for ants and beetles beneath the bark of trees

_____

1 mark

d) fly at high speeds.

_____

1 mark

5 Animals that live in the polar regions have to be able to survive in very cold conditions.

Give two ways in which this polar bear has adapted in order to live in these conditions.

_____

_____

_____

2 marks

MATERIALS & THEIR PROPERTIES

The structure of solids, liquids and gases

Scientists believe that **solids**, **liquids** and **gases** are made up of extremely small **particles** – they are so small it is impossible to see them, even with a strong microscope. These particles are arranged differently in solids, liquids and gases. It is these arrangements which give rise to the different properties.

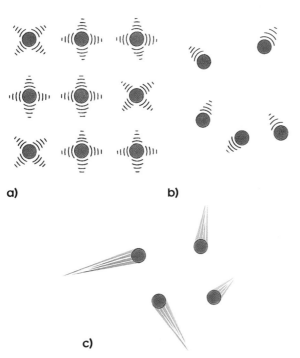

Figure 1 **The arrangement of particles** in a) a solid, b) a liquid and c) a gas

In solids the particles are a) close together, b) in layers, c) in fixed positions but are able to **vibrate** from side to side, and d) held together by strong forces.

In liquids the particles are a) a little further apart than the particles of a solid, b) not in fixed positions but are able to move around a little and c) held together by weaker forces than the particles in a solid.

In gases the particles are a) far apart, b) completely free to move around within their container and c) not held together by any forces.

The properties of solids, liquids and gases

Shape

Solids have a definite shape.

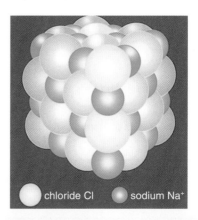

chloride Cl   sodium Na⁺

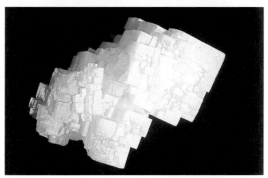

Figure 2 Crystal structures **like this form because the particles in solids are arranged in layers**

Liquids do not have a definite shape.

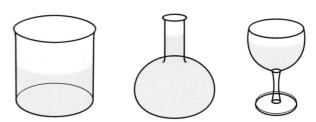

Figure 3 **The particles in a liquid are not in fixed positions so it can take the shape of the container**

Gases do not have a definite shape.

Figure 4 **Gas particles are completely free and will fill any container into which they are placed**

The strengths of solids, liquids and gases

Because of the strong forces between the particles, solids are **firm** and can support things. Liquids and gases have no **strength** or firmness.

The ability to flow

Because the forces between the particles in liquids and gases are weak or non-existent, they are able to **flow**. The strong forces between the particles in solids prevent them from flowing.

Squashability!

Because their particles are far apart, gases can be squashed. The particles of solids and liquids are close together and they are therefore not easily squashed.

Diffusion

The particles of liquids and gases are able to move and mix. This mixing is called **diffusion**.

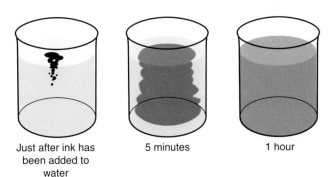

| Just after ink has been added to water | 5 minutes | 1 hour |

Figure 5 **The drop of ink gradually spreads through the beaker by the motion of the water particles**

Key terms

Check that you understand and can explain the following terms:

★ solid
★ liquid
★ gas
★ particle
★ arrangement of particles
★ vibrate

★ crystal structure
★ firmness
★ strength
★ flow
★ diffusion
★ pressure of a gas

Questions

1 Draw three labelled diagrams to show how the particles are arranged in a) a solid, b) a liquid and c) a gas.

2 Name three materials/substances whose particles are close together.

3 Name three materials/substances whose particles are free to move around.

4 Name three materials/substances that can not easily be squashed.

5 What is the name of the process by which the smell of food spreads around a kitchen?

6 Draw a diagram to show how the air particles inside a balloon create pressure.

Gas pressure

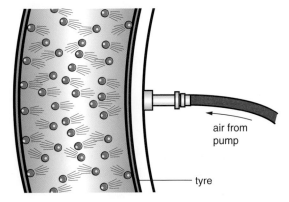

air from pump

tyre

Figure 6 **The gas particles inside this tyre are continually bouncing off the sides. It is these collisions which create the** pressure **inside the tyre**

If more air is pumped into the tyre there will be more particles and more collisions, so the pressure in the tyre will increase.

6.2 MELTING AND BOILING

Melting

If a solid is heated gently its particles vibrate more and more vigorously. Eventually they vibrate so violently that the layered structure breaks apart and the particles are able to move around. The temperature at which this happens is called the **melting point** of the solid. The solid has now become a liquid.

If a liquid is cooled to below its melting point the layered structure reforms and becomes a solid once again. The liquid has **solidified** or **frozen**.

Boiling

If a liquid is heated, the vibrations may become so violent that the particles become completely free. The temperature at which this happens is called the **boiling point** of the liquid. The liquid has now become a gas.

If a gas is cooled to a temperature below its boiling point, the groups of particles reform and the gas changes into a liquid. The gas has **condensed**.

Graphs showing changes of state with temperature are given on page 72.

The table below gives some examples of the melting points and boiling points of different materials.

Substance	Melting point °C	Boiling point °C
Water	0	100
Alcohol	−117	78
Tungsten	3410	5500
Iron	1539	2887
Oxygen	−219	−183

Figure 1 **Iron has a high melting point. It melts at a temperature of 1539°C**

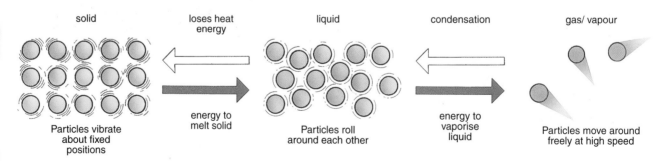

Figure 2 **Changes of state**

Figure 3 **We normally think of nitrogen as being a gas, but if it is cooled to below a temperature of −196°C, it becomes a liquid**

Key terms

Check that you understand and can explain the following terms:

* to melt
* melting point
* to solidify
* to freeze

* to boil
* boiling point
* to condense

Questions

1 Explain what happens to the structure of a solid when it melts.

2 Explain what happens to the structure of a liquid when it boils.

3 Explain the differences a) between melting and freezing, and b) between boiling and condensing.

4 Look carefully at the table below then answer the questions.

Material	Melting point °C	Boiling point °C
Water	0	100
Common salt	801	1420
Copper	1083	2582
Iron	1539	2887

a) What happens to common salt at i) 801°C and ii) 1420°C?

b) How are the particles arranged in iron at 1400°C?

c) What happens to water if its temperature changes from 120°C to 80°C?

d) Explain in detail what happens to the particles in a sample of copper if its temperature is increased from 1000°C to 1200°C.

Figure 4 **The photograph above shows droplets of liquid mercury**

Mercury is the only metal which is a liquid at room temperature. It freezes at −38.8°C and boils at 356.9°C. Why are mercury thermometers not used to measure temperatures in the Arctic and Antarctic?

ATOMS, ELEMENTS AND THE PERIODIC TABLE

CLASSIFYING MATERIALS (1)

Everything on the Earth is made from tiny particles called **atoms**. Inside each atom are even smaller particles called **protons**, **neutrons** and **electrons**. The protons and neutrons are in the centre of the atom, the **nucleus**. The electrons **orbit** the centre of the atom in a similar way to the way that planets orbit the Sun. There are usually the same number of protons and electrons in an atom.

Altogether there are approximately 95 naturally-occurring **elements**. These are shown here in a special table called the **periodic table**. The elements are arranged in the table in such a way that elements which have a similar electronic structure and similar properties are in the same part of the table. For example, the elements on the far right of the table – neon, argon, krypton, xenon and radon – are all gases and are very unreactive. The elements on the far left – including lithium, sodium and potassium – are the alkali metals and are very reactive.

The table opposite lists some of the more common elements and their **symbols**. (You don't have to memorize them – the symbols are just a kind of shorthand for the names of the elements.)

Figure 1 **Structure of a magnesium atom**

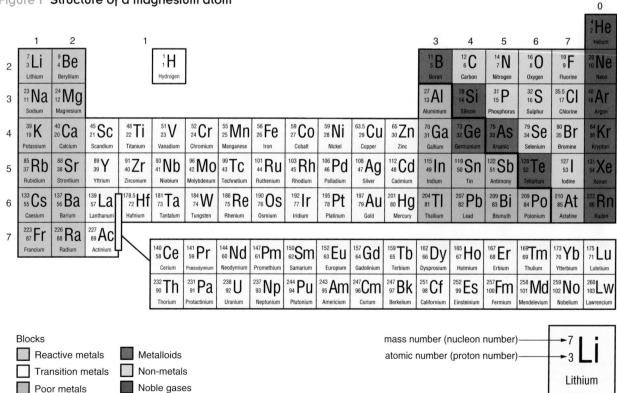

Figure 2 **The periodic table**

Element	Symbol	Element	Symbol
hydrogen	H	sulphur	S
helium	He	chlorine	Cl
lithium	Li	calcium	Ca
carbon	C	iron	Fe
nitrogen	N	copper	Cu
oxygen	O	zinc	Zn
sodium	Na	silver	Ag
magnesium	Mg	gold	Au
aluminium	Al	lead	Pb

Atomic structure

All atoms of an element contain the same number of protons.

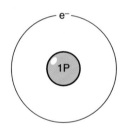

Figure 3 A hydrogen atom

Hydrogen is element number one in the periodic table because a hydrogen atom contains just one proton in its nucleus. All atoms of hydrogen have just one proton in their nuclei.

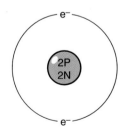

Figure 4 A helium atom

Helium is element number two in the periodic table because a helium atom contains two protons in its nucleus. All atoms of helium have two protons in their nuclei.

Key terms

Check that you understand and can explain the following terms:

* atom
* proton
* neutron
* electron
* nucleus

* orbit
* element
* periodic table
* symbol

Questions

1 Write down the symbols for the following elements:

   a) helium, b) calcium, c) aluminium, d) silicon and e) cobalt.

2 Which elements have the following symbols:

   a) Cu, b) Fe, c) C, d) O and e) Pb?

3 How many protons do the following have in their nuclei:

   a) bromine (Br), b) iodine (I), c) platinum (Pt) and d) tin (Sn)?

4 Write down an element which has a similar structure and similar properties to each of the following:

   a) neon (Ne), b) sodium (Na) and c) calcium (Ca).

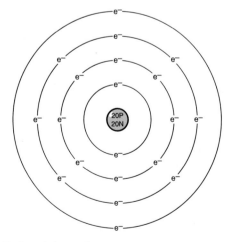

Figure 5 A calcium atom

Calcium is element number 20 in the periodic table because a calcium atom contains 20 protons in its nucleus. All calcium atoms have 20 protons in their nuclei.

What you need to know!

1   Solids, liquids and gases have different physical properties, for example shape, strength and ability to flow.

2   These different properties can be explained by the arrangement and movement of their particles.

3   When a substance melts, the arrangement and movement of its particles change.

4   Elements consist of atoms. The atoms of the same element contain the same number of protons.

5   The periodic table contains all the elements, their symbols and the number of protons each element has in its nucleus.

6   Elements which have similar electronic structures/similar chemical properties are placed near each other in the periodic table.

How much do you know?

1   This question is about the different properties of solids, liquids and gases.

◆   Iron is a solid at room temperature
◆   Water is a liquid at room temperature
◆   Oxygen is a gas at room temperature

a)   In which substance are the particles completely free to move around at room temperature?

_____

1 mark

b)   In which substance are the particles arranged in a regular pattern at room temperature?

_____

1 mark

c)   In which substance are the forces of attraction between the particles strongest at room temperature?

_____

1 mark

d)   Which substance may condense if it is cooled down?

_____

1 mark

e)   Which substance may melt if its temperature is increased?

_____

1 mark

f)   Which two substances can be poured?

_____

_____

2 marks

2   This question is about the melting points and boiling points of five substances.

Substance	Melting point °C	Boiling point °C
A	0	100
B	−20	78
C	1000	2000
D	−180	−10
E	80	300

Using the information in the table above answer the following questions.

a)   Is substance A a solid, liquid or gas when it is at a temperature of 50°C?

_____

1 mark

b)   Is substance B a solid, liquid or gas when it is at a temperature of 10°C?

_____

1 mark

c)   Is substance C a solid, liquid or gas when it is at a temperature of 50°C?

_____

1 mark

d)   Is substance D a solid, liquid or gas when it is at a temperature of 50°C?

_____

1 mark

How much do you know? continued

e) Is substance E a solid, liquid or gas when it is at a temperature of 50°C?

_____

1 mark

f) Which two substances have a regular structure at 10°C?

_____

_____

2 marks

3 A solid X was heated for 40 minutes. Its temperature was taken every minute. The graph below shows how its temperature changed with time.

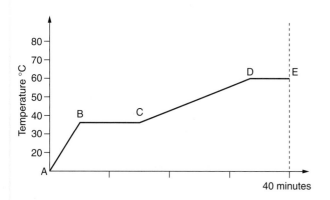

a) What happened to solid X between B and C?

_____

1 mark

b) What happened to X between D and E?

_____

1 mark

c) Describe the arrangement of the particles in X between C and D.

_____

_____

2 marks

d) Tick one box in each column to describe the forces of attraction between the particles in a solid, liquid and gas.

Forces between particles	Solid	Liquid	Gas
No forces			
Very strong forces			

3 marks

4 Using the periodic table on page 58 answer the following questions.

a) Name two elements that have similar properties to Na (sodium).

_____

2 marks

b) Name two elements that have similar properties to Ne (neon).

_____

2 marks

c) All atoms of the same element contain the same number of protons. How many protons are there in an atom of

i)   H (hydrogen)? _____   *1 mark*
ii) Na (sodium)? _____   *1 mark*
iii) C (carbon)? _____   *1 mark*

6.4 COMPOUNDS, MIXTURES AND SOLUTIONS

A **pure substance** contains just one element or compound.

Figure 1 **This ring is made from pure gold. It contains only gold atoms**

A **mixture** contains more than one element or compound.

Figure 2 **This bowl contains the different ingredients needed to make a cake – including eggs, flour, margarine and sugar. It is a mixture**

The air we breathe is a mixture of different gases, including nitrogen, oxygen and carbon dioxide.

Certain substances, such as sugar and salt, dissolve in water to form a special kind of mixture called a **solution**.

Figure 3 **The substance which has dissolved is called the** solute. **The liquid into which it has dissolved is called the** solvent. **The mixture of solute and solvent is called the** solution

A **compound** is a pure substance formed when two or more elements combine together chemically.

The differences between compounds and mixtures

1 In general it is much easier to separate the different substances in a mixture than to separate the substances in a compound.

Separating mixtures

Filtering
A mixture such as sand and water can be separated by **filtering**. The water passes through the filter paper but the sand cannot.

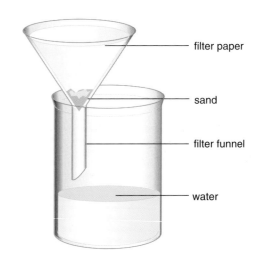

Figure 4 **The separation of sand from water**

Dissolving and filtering
A mixture of sand and salt can be separated by dissolving the salt and filtering away the sand, as salt is soluble in the water but sand is not.

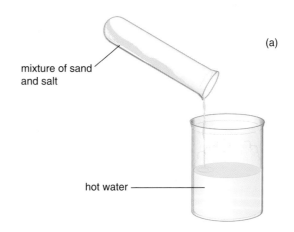

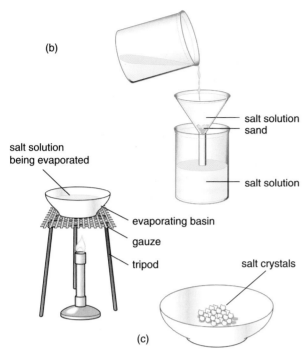

(b)

salt solution
sand

salt solution
being evaporated

salt solution

evaporating basin

gauze

tripod

salt crystals

(c)

Figure 5

a) **Adding the mixture to water in order to dissolve the salt**
b) **Filtering the mixture to remove the sand**
c) **Heating the solution so that the water evaporates leaving the salt (solid)**

Distilling

A mixture of two liquids which have different boiling points, for example water (100°C) and alcohol (78°C), can be separated by **distillation**. When the mixture is heated, the liquid with the lower boiling point boils first. It travels as a vapour along the condenser where it is cooled and changes back into a liquid which is collected in a beaker. The liquid with the higher boiling point remains in the flask.

Chromatography

A mixture of two or more liquids can often be separated using a technique called **chromatography**. Inks are often mixtures of several dyes (liquids). You can show this by separating the different dyes using the technique described below.

A small drop of ink is placed on a piece of filter paper. The paper is then suspended over a beaker of water (the solvent). As the water rises, the different dyes within the ink are carried different distances up the paper. The most soluble dye travels furthest.

filter paper

water has risen
to this level

ink spot

B

A

beaker

original ink spot
(almost invisible)

Figure 7 Chromatography

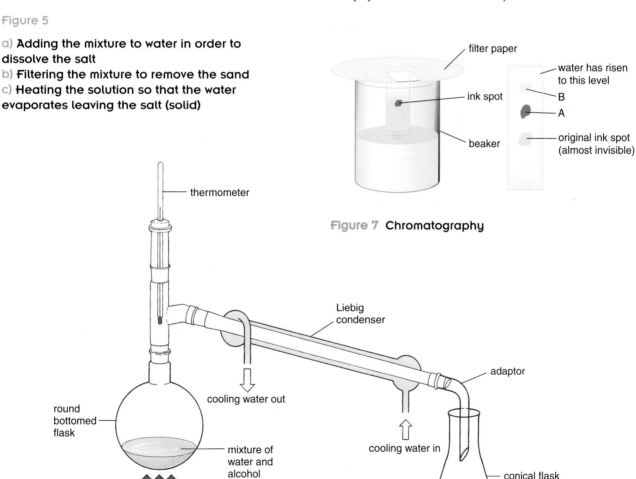

thermometer

Liebig
condenser

adaptor

cooling water out

round
bottomed
flask

mixture of
water and
alcohol

cooling water in

conical flask

Heat gently

alcohol

Figure 6 Distillation

2 The properties of mixtures tend to be similar to those of the substances which have been mixed together. The properties of a compound are generally totally different from those of the substances from which it is made.

For example, sodium is an extremely reactive metal. If it is placed in water it will react very violently. Any contact between sodium metal and skin would be very dangerous. Chlorine is a yellowish, poisonous gas.

When sodium and chlorine join they form a solid, white, crystalline compound called sodium chloride. This compound is the common salt which we find dissolved in the sea and which we sprinkle on our food.

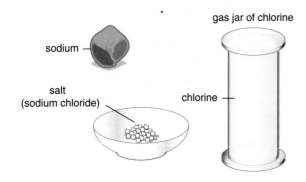

Figure 8 **Sodium, chlorine and salt**

This joining together of substances to form new compounds is called a **chemical reaction**. This **chemical change** can be written as a **word equation**.

sodium + chlorine → sodium chloride (salt)

If yellow sulphur is heated with iron filings there is a chemical reaction and a compound called iron sulphide is formed. This compound has properties which are totally different from those of the sulphur and the iron from which it is formed.

iron + sulphur → iron sulphide

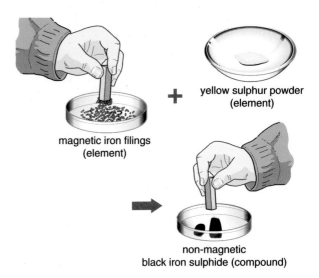

Figure 9 **Iron filings, sulphur and iron sulphide**

3 Compounds have a definite composition. Mixtures do not have a definite composition.

When you want to sweeten a cup of tea or coffee you add sugar. How much sugar you add depends upon your taste. You can do this because sugar dissolves in a liquid to form a mixture. You can decide how much of each substance is present.

When substances react together to produce compounds the correct amount of each must be present.

When iron reacts with sulphur to produce the compound iron sulphide there must be equal numbers of iron atoms and sulphur atoms.

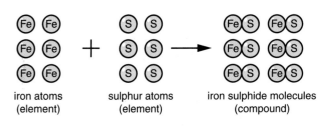

Figure 10 **Equal numbers of iron and sulphur atoms react to produce iron sulphide**

When carbon reacts with oxygen to produce the compound carbon dioxide there must be two oxygen atoms for every carbon atom.

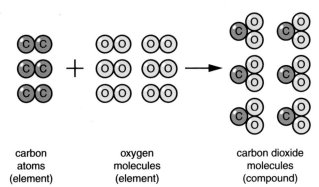

carbon
atoms
(element)

oxygen
molecules
(element)

carbon dioxide
molecules
(compound)

Figure 11 **Carbon reacts with twice as many oxygen atoms to produce carbon dioxide**

When nitrogen reacts with hydrogen to produce ammonia there must be three hydrogen atoms for each nitrogen atom.

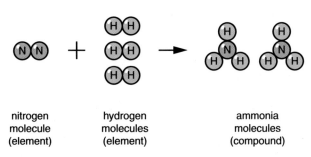

nitrogen
molecule
(element)

hydrogen
molecules
(element)

ammonia
molecules
(compound)

Figure 12 **Nitrogen reacts with three times as many hydrogen atoms to produce ammonia**

Chemical formulae

Because compounds have a definite composition it is possible to describe them using a chemical formula. Some examples of compounds and their chemical formulae are shown below.

Name	Composition	Chemical formula
sodium chloride	one sodium (Na) atom for each chlorine (Cl) atom	NaCl
iron sulphide	one iron (Fe) atom for each sulphur (S) atom	FeS
carbon dioxide	two oxygen (O) atoms for each carbon (C) atom	CO_2
water	two hydrogen (H) atoms for each oxygen (O) atom	H_2O
ammonia	three hydrogen (H) atoms for each nitrogen (N) atom	NH_3

Key terms

Check that you understand and can explain the following terms:

* pure substance
* mixture
* solution
* solute
* solvent
* compound

* filter
* distill
* chromatography
* chemical reaction
* chemical change
* word equation

Questions

1 What is a) a pure substance, b) a mixture, c) a compound? Give one example of each.

2 What are the three main differences between a compound and a mixture?

3 Explain how you could separate the following mixtures
a) rice and water, b) rice and salt.

4 How could you prove that an ink contains more than one dye?

5 Give one example of a compound which has totally different properties from the substances from which it is made.

6 Complete the table below

Name	Composition	Chemical formula
magnesium chloride		$MgCl_2$
calcium oxide	one calcium (Ca) atom for each oxygen (O) atom	
carbon monoxide	one oxygen (O) atom for each carbon (C) atom	
sulphur trioxide	three sulphur (S) atoms for each oxygen (O) atom	
aluminium chloride		$AlCl_3$

	1													3	4	5	6	7	0
							¹₁H Hydrogen												⁴₂He Helium
2	⁷₃Li Lithium	⁹₄Be Beryllium												¹¹₅B Boron	¹²₆C Carbon	¹⁴₇N Nitrogen	¹⁶₈O Oxygen	¹⁹₉F Fluorine	²⁰₁₀Ne Neon
3	²³₁₁Na Sodium	²⁴₁₂Mg Magnesium												²⁷₁₃Al Aluminium	²⁸₁₄Si Silicon	³¹₁₅P Phosphorus	³²₁₆S Sulphur	³⁵·⁵₁₇Cl Chlorine	⁴⁰₁₈Ar Argon
4	³⁹₁₉K Potassium	⁴⁰₂₀Ca Calcium	⁴⁵₂₁Sc Scandium	⁴⁸₂₂Ti Titanium	⁵¹₂₃V Vanadium	⁵²₂₄Cr Chromium	⁵⁵₂₅Mn Manganese	⁵⁶₂₆Fe Iron	⁵⁹₂₇Co Cobalt	⁵⁹₂₈Ni Nickel	⁶³·⁵₂₉Cu Copper	⁶⁵₃₀Zn Zinc	⁷⁰₃₁Ga Gallium	⁷³₃₂Ge Germanium	⁷⁵₃₃As Arsenic	⁷⁹₃₄Se Selenium	⁸⁰₃₅Br Bromine	⁸⁴₃₆Kr Krypton
5	⁸⁵₃₇Rb Rubidium	⁸⁸₃₈Sr Strontium	⁸⁹₃₉Y Yttrium	⁹¹₄₀Zr Zirconium	⁹³₄₁Nb Niobium	⁹⁶₄₂Mo Molybdenum	⁹⁹₄₃Tc Technetium	¹⁰¹₄₄Ru Ruthenium	¹⁰³₄₅Rh Rhodium	¹⁰⁶₄₆Pd Palladium	¹⁰⁸₄₇Ag Silver	¹¹²₄₈Cd Cadmium	¹¹⁵₄₉In Indium	¹¹⁹₅₀Sn Tin	¹²²₅₁Sb Antimony	¹²⁸₅₂Te Tellurium	¹²⁷₅₃I Iodine	¹³¹₅₄Xe Xenon
6	¹³³₅₅Cs Caesium	¹³⁷₅₆Ba Barium	¹³⁹₅₇La Lanthanum	¹⁷⁸·⁵₇₂Hf Hafnium	¹⁸¹₇₃Ta Tantalum	¹⁸⁴₇₄W Tungsten	¹⁸⁶₇₅Re Rhenium	¹⁹⁰₇₆Os Osmium	¹⁹²₇₇Ir Iridium	¹⁹⁵₇₈Pt Platinum	¹⁹⁷₇₉Au Gold	²⁰¹₈₀Hg Mercury	²⁰⁴₈₁Tl Thallium	²⁰⁷₈₂Pb Lead	²⁰⁹₈₃Bi Bismuth	²⁰⁹₈₄Po Polonium	²¹⁰₈₅At Astatine	²²²₈₆Rn Radon
7	²²³₈₇Fr Francium	²²⁶₈₈Ra Radium	²²⁷₈₉Ac Actinium															

Blocks
☐ Metals
▨ Non-metals

Figure 1 **All of the elements in the periodic table are either metals or non-metals**

The **physical** and **chemical properties** of an element determine whether it is a metal or a non-metal.

Physical properties of metals

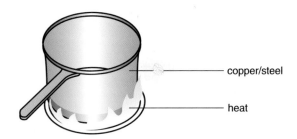

Figure 2 **All metals are** good conductors of heat

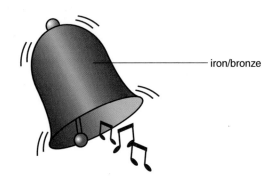

Figure 3 **Most metal objects produce a ringing 'metallic' sound when struck**

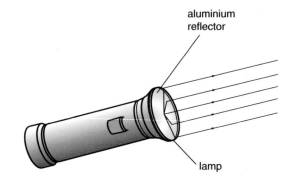

Figure 4 **Most metals have a shiny appearance**

Figure 5 **Metals are flexible and** ductile

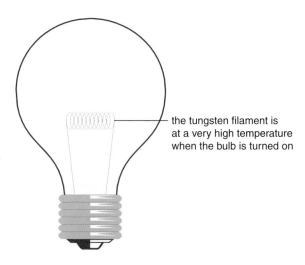

Figure 6 Most metals have a high melting point and boiling point

the tungsten filament is at a very high temperature when the bulb is turned on

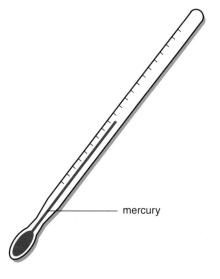

mercury

Figure 8 Mercury is the only metal which is a liquid at room temperature. When the mercury inside the thermometer warms it expands, showing the new temperature. When the liquid cools, it contracts

iron horsehoe

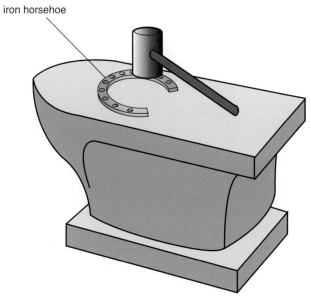

Figure 7 Most metals can be hammered into shape. They are malleable

Figure 9 Most metals are dense. A small amount of them weighs a lot

Figure 10 **Metals are strong**

Figure 11 **All metals are good conductors of electricity**

Physical properties of non-metals

The physical properties of non-metals vary widely and, unlike the metals, show few trends. For example, at room temperature many non-metals are gases, some are solids and one is a liquid.

Sulphur is a yellow solid at room temperature

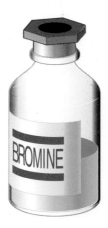

Bromine is a red-brown liquid at room temperature

Chlorine is a yellowish gas at room temperature

Figure 12

Key terms

Check that you understand and can explain the following terms:

* physical property
* chemical property
* good conductors of heat/electricity
* ductile
* malleable
* dense

Question

1 To which group do the following materials belong.
   a) Material A is a poor conductor of heat.
   b) Material B makes a ringing sound when struck.
   c) Material C is a gas at room temperature.
   d) Material D is shiny.
   e) Material E is malleable.
   f) Material F has a low density.
   g) Material G is magnetic.

Summary

Property	Metals	Non-metals
State	Nearly all solids	Can be solid, liquid or gas
Appearance	Mostly shiny	Very varied
Strength	Strong	Generally weak
Density	Mostly high	Generally low
Melting/ boiling points	Mostly high	Generally low
Conduction of heat	Very good	Poor
Conduction of electricity	Very good	Poor

What you need to know!

1 A compound is created when elements combine together chemically.

2 A mixture contains elements or compounds which are not joined together chemically.

3 Compounds have a definite composition, mixtures do not.

4 Mixtures may be separated by filtration, distillation or chromatography.

5 The ingredients of compounds cannot easily be separated.

6 Most metals are shiny solids at room temperature.

7 Metals are good conductors of heat and electricity.

8 A few metals are magnetic.

9 Non-metals may be solids, liquids or gases at room temperature.

10 Non-metals are poor conductors of heat and electricity.

How much do you know?

1 John adds a teaspoon of coffee to some hot water and stirs it until it has dissolved. Describe how John could now separate the coffee from the water.

_____

_____

_____

2 marks

2 The diagram below shows how a mixture of sand and salt can be separated by filtering.

a) Where is the sand after the mixture has been filtered?

_____

1 mark

b) Where is the salt after it has been filtered?

_____

1 mark

c) Explain why it would not be possible to separate a mixture of salt and sugar by adding them to water and then filtering.

_____

_____

2 marks

3 The diagram below shows the apparatus that is used to separate two liquids such as water and alcohol.

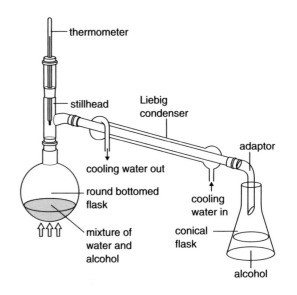

How much do you know? continued

Water has a boiling point of 100°C. Alcohol has a boiling point of 78°C.

a) What happens to the alcohol when the mixture is heated to a temperature of 78°C?

_____
1 mark

b) What happens to any alcohol vapour which passes through the condenser?

_____
1 mark

4 A forensic scientist is trying to discover which pen was used to write a false cheque. Using chromatography he was able to compare the ink from the cheque with that from three pens. The results are shown below.

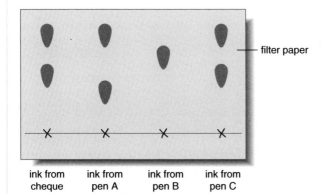

ink from   ink from   ink from   ink from
cheque   pen A   pen B   pen C

filter paper

a) Which pen was used to write the cheque?

_____
1 mark

b) Explain how the scientist was able to decide this.

_____
2 marks

5 a) What is formed when there is a chemical reaction between two or more substances?

_____
1 mark

b) What is formed when a solid is dissolved in a liquid?

_____
1 mark

c) What kind of change takes place when all the ingredients for a cake are mixed and put into an oven.

_____
1 mark

6 Put each of the properties listed below in the correct column of the table.

strong
brittle
flexible
shiny
low melting point
good conductor of heat
low density
poor conductor of electricity

Property of a metal	Property of a non-metal

8 marks

7 The table below gives the name and chemical composition of some compounds.

Write the chemical formula for each compound in the third column. The first one has been done for you.

Name of compound	Composition of compound	Chemical formula
sodium chloride	one atom of sodium (Na) plus one atom of chlorine (Cl)	NaCl
carbon dioxide	one atom of carbon (C) plus two atoms of oxygen (O)	
water	two atoms of hydrogen (H) plus one atom of oxygen	

2 marks

7.1 PHYSICAL CHANGES

Using the right materials

Different materials have different useful properties. It is important to choose the right material for the job.

The materials used to build this cottage were chosen because of their **physical properties**.

Figure 1

Natural materials are often changed in some way before they are used. Fibres such as cotton and wool may be spun and then woven. If wood is crushed, rolled and dried it can be made into paper. Wood and stone may be worked into a particular shape. All these changes are **physical changes**.

A physical change is one which

◆ is usually easy to **reverse**
◆ makes no new substance.

More examples of physical changes

1 Changing state – melting, boiling and freezing

If a solid such as a piece of ice is heated, it takes in energy. The graph below shows how the temperature and the state of the ice changes with time.

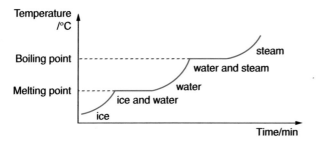

Figure 2 Changes of state **as water is heated**

Because these are physical changes, they are easy to reverse. If the steam is allowed to cool, it loses energy. The graph below shows how the temperature and state of the steam changes with time.

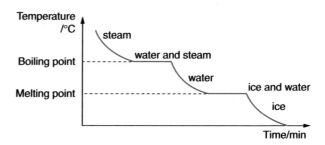

Figure 3 **Changes of state as water is cooled**

2 Dissolving

The amount of solid that can be dissolved in a liquid depends upon

◆ the liquid (solvent) used
◆ its temperature.

The warmer the solvent, the more solid it can dissolve.

If you add a teaspoon of sugar to a cup of tea, the sugar disappears as it dissolves.

The sugar in the above example can be reclaimed by gently boiling the water away.

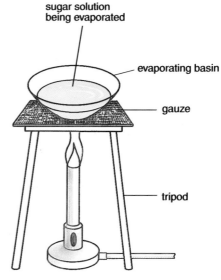

Figure 4 **The apparatus used to reclaim the dissolved sugar**

3 Thermal expansion and contraction

When an object is heated its **particles vibrate** more vigorously and the object **expands**.

When an object cools, the vibrations of its particles become less vigorous and the object **contracts**.

(a)
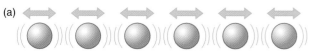
After heating

(b)
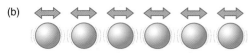
After cooling

Figure 5 **Expansion and contraction of a solid**

The Firth of Forth railway bridge is approximately 1 metre longer in the summer than it is in the winter. This change in length had to be taken into account when the bridge was constructed.

When objects expand and contract they can exert very large forces. There are occasions when these large forces can be used to our advantage.

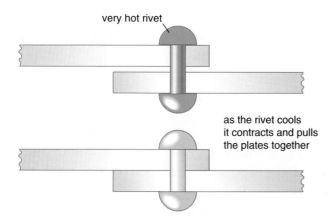
very hot rivet

as the rivet cools it contracts and pulls the plates together

Figure 6 **As the rivet cools down it contracts, pulling the two plates together. The force with which it does this is so strong that the joint is watertight**

Key terms

Check that you understand and can explain the following terms:

* physical property
* natural material
* physical change
* reverse
* change state
* particle
* vibrate
* thermal expansion
* thermal contraction

Questions

1 Select five objects from your room. Write down the material each object is made from and suggest one reason why that material was used.

2 What are the two main features of a physical change?

3 Which of the following are physical changes? Explain your answers.
   a) mixing salt and sand
   b) baking a cake
   c) dissolving coffee in hot water
   d) burning a piece of paper.

4 Give one use of thermal expansion and contraction.

5 Give one disadvantage of thermal expansion and contraction.

CHANGING MATERIALS (1)

7.2 GEOLOGICAL CHANGES

The structure of the Earth

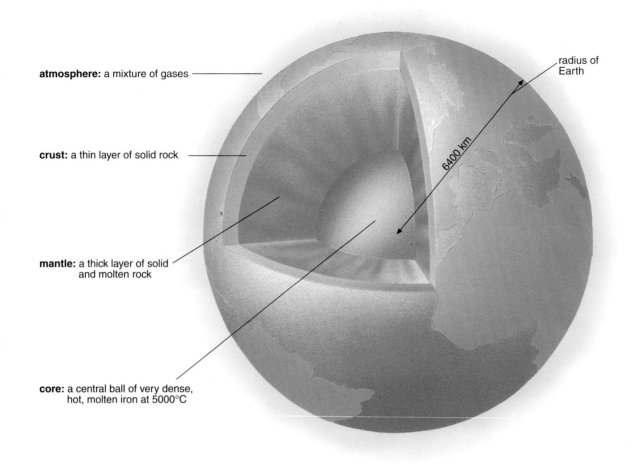

atmosphere: a mixture of gases

crust: a thin layer of solid rock

mantle: a thick layer of solid and molten rock

core: a central ball of very dense, hot, molten iron at 5000°C

radius of Earth

6400 km

Figure 1 **The structure of the Earth**

The solid outer layer of the Earth is called the crust. In some areas the crust is very thin (16 km) whilst in others it is nearly 100 km thick.

The mantle is mainly solid rocks but the high temperatures and pressures in this layer mean that they behave like an extremely thick liquid and are able to move around very slowly.

The core is the hottest part of the Earth. Temperatures reach approximately 5000°C at its centre.

Within the crust of the Earth there are three main types of rocks – **igneous**, **sedimentary** and **metamorphic**. These rocks are continuously being created, destroyed and then recreated over a period of millions of years. These **geological changes** are called the **rock cycle**.

The rock cycle

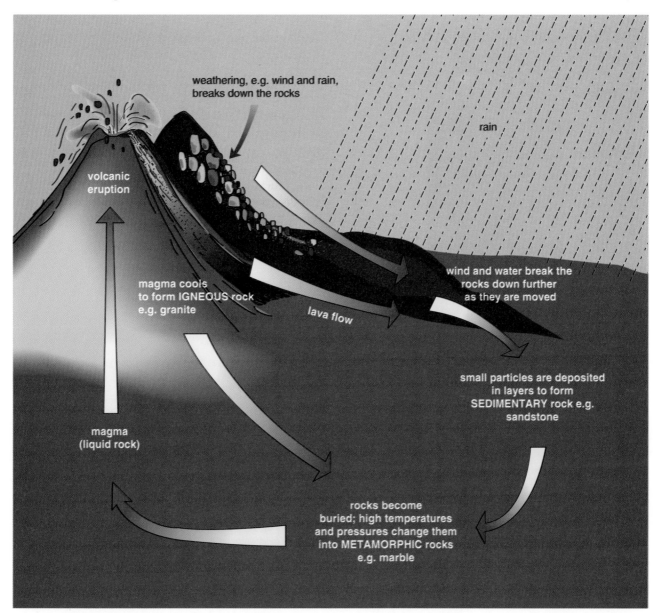

Figure 2 **The rock cycle**

Formation of igneous rocks

When a volcano erupts, the high pressures on the rocks below are released and the rocks change into a liquid. This **liquid rock** is called **magma**. Liquid rock which escapes from the volcano and flows down its sides is called **lava**. When the liquid rock cools and solidifies, igneous rocks such as granite and basalt are formed.

The igneous rocks formed contain crystals. If the magma cools slowly the crystals have time to grow and are quite large. If the magma cools rapidly the crystals will be quite small. This is important because the strength and hardness of these rocks depends upon the size of their crystals.

CHANGING MATERIALS (1)

Formation of sedimentary rocks

All rocks on the surface of the Earth change because of the effects of the weather. This process is called **weathering**.

Figure 3 **Rain and running water can wear away rocks. The wearing away of the rock surface is called** erosion. **The faster the water moves, the faster the erosion.**

Acids in the atmosphere (see Acid Rain p 94) may lead to chemical weathering of rocks

Weathering will gradually break rocks down into small particles. These small particles are then **transported** by rivers and winds. Eventually they come to rest and are **deposited**. Over a long period of time other layers of particles settle on top of them. The lower layers become squashed and eventually form a new type of rock with a layered structure. This rock is called sedimentary rock. Limestone and sandstone are sedimentary rocks.

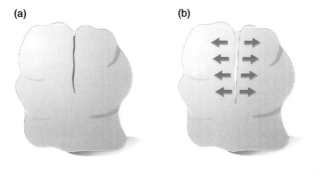

(a) (b)

a) Water seeps into a crack in the rock

b) The water freezes, expands and forces the pieces of rock apart

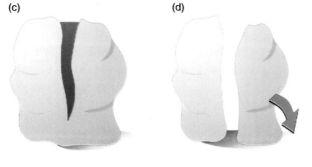

(c) (d)

c) The ice thaws and water seeps further into the crack

d) Further freezing and thawing occurs and eventually a piece of rock breaks off

Figure 4 **The physical weathering of rock by water**

Figure 5 **The layers of sedimentary rock are clearly visible in this limestone quarry**

Formation of metamorphic rocks

Rocks which are deep in the ground or are close to erupting volcanoes may change in structure due to the high pressures and temperatures they experience. These new structures are the third kind of rock – called metamorphic rocks. When limestone experiences high temperatures and pressures it changes into marble. Mudstone, under the same conditions, will change into slate.

Figure 6 **Slate is often used for roofing and floors of buildings**

Rocks have many important uses. They can be used for the walls and roofs of houses, for the floors and pillars of large buildings and in the manufacture of plaster and cement. The different properties of the various kinds of rock will determine which is used for which purpose.

Key terms

Check that you understand and can explain the following terms:

- ★ igneous rock
- ★ sedimentary rock
- ★ metamorphic rock
- ★ geological changes
- ★ rock cycle
- ★ liquid rock/magma
- ★ lava
- ★ weathering
- ★ erosion
- ★ transport
- ★ deposit

Questions

1 Draw a simple diagram of the structure of the Earth. Label the main parts.

2 What is magma? What is lava?

3 Name two igneous rocks.

4 Explain how large rocks might be broken down into very small particles by the weather.

5 Why might a visit to a quarry confirm our ideas of how sedimentary rocks are formed? Name two sedimentary rocks.

6 Name one metamorphic rock. Give one use for this type of rock.

Rock	Description	Uses
Granite	Very hard	Building stone
Sandstone	Very hard	Building stone
Limestone	Light colour	Making cement
Marble	Hard, smooth	Statues, floors
Slate	Hard, waterproof	Roofing tiles

What you need to know!

1 When physical changes take place, for example changes of state, there is no change in mass.

2 The amount of solid that will dissolve depends upon the liquid used and its temperature.

3 When materials change state they either gain or lose energy.

4 Most materials expand when heated and contract when cooled.

5 Rocks are continually being changed within the rock cycle.

6 There are three main types of rock with different physical properties. They are sedimentary rocks, metamorphic rocks and igneous rocks.

How much do you know?

1 Use these words to complete the sentences below.

increases   decreases   remains the same

gives out   takes in

Each of these words or phrases may be used once, more than once or not at all.

a) When ice melts it _____ energy. Its mass _____ .

b) When water freezes it _____ energy. Its mass _____ .

4 marks

2 The graph below shows how the temperature of a piece of ice changes when it is heated.

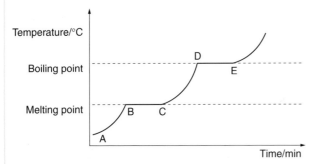

a) What is happening to the ice between points B and C?

_____

1 mark

b) What is happening between points D and E?

_____

1 mark

The four statements below describe how molecules may move.

A – The molecules are completely free to move
B – The molecules just vibrate from side to side
C – The molecules are able to move around a little
D – The molecules move in straight lines

c) Choose the one statement which describes the behaviour of the molecules between points A and B on the graph.

_____

1 mark

d) Choose the one statement which describes the behaviour of the molecules between points C and D on the graph.

_____

1 mark

3 Richard put some sugar in a cup of cold water. After a few minutes all the sugar dissolved. Suggest two ways in which Richard could make the sugar dissolve more quickly.

_____

_____

2 marks

4 The diagram opposite shows a metal ball and a metal ring.

When both the ball and ring are at room temperature the ball can pass through the ring.

a) Explain why the ball is unable to pass through the ring when it has been heated for several minutes with a Bunsen burner.

_____

2 marks

How much do you know? continued

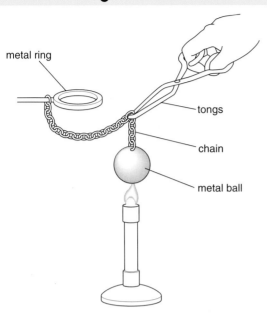

metal ring

tongs

chain

metal ball

b) Explain why the ball can once again pass through the ring when the apparatus is left on the desk for several more minutes.

_____

2 marks

5 Rocks can be classified into three groups – igneous rocks, sedimentary rocks and metamorphic rocks.

Look carefully at the information opposite and decide to which group each of the four different rocks A, B, C and D belongs.

Rock	Description	Group
A	Has a layered structure and contains pieces of shell	
B	Very hard, glassy, smooth appearance	
C	Has a crystalline structure but no layers can be seen	
D	Hard but is easily split into thin layers	

4 marks

6 a) The diagram below shows the rock cycle.

Choose three words from this list to complete the labelling of the diagram.

weathering   deposition   transport   melting

3 marks

b) What two conditions are necessary to change a sedimentary rock into a metamorphic rock?

_____

_____

2 marks

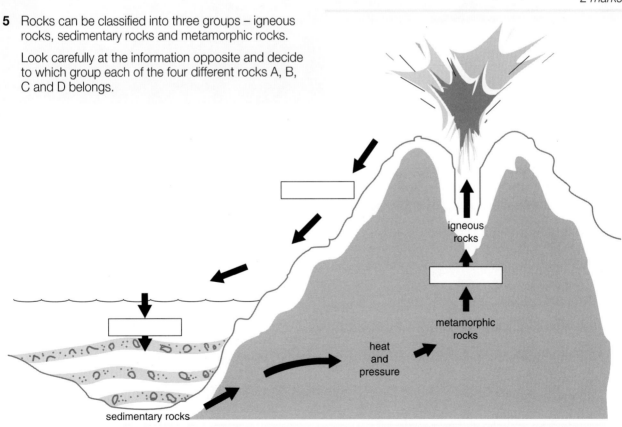

igneous rocks

metamorphic rocks

heat and pressure

sedimentary rocks

CHEMICAL CHANGES

Many of the objects you can see in this photograph are not made from natural materials. The china, the metals and the fibres from which they are made have been produced by **chemical reactions**. The **raw materials** have been chemically changed.

Figure 1

The cups, saucers and plates are made from china clay. When it is heated, a chemical reaction takes place and the soft, wet clay changes into a hard solid.

The metal from which the knives, forks and spoons are made is not found as a raw material in the ground. It is found as an ore which is then chemically changed to produce the metal.

The plastic fibres used to manufacture the table cloth are made from chemicals found in oil.

A **chemical change** is one which

◆ is difficult to reverse
◆ forms a new substance.

There are many examples of useful chemical changes. Chemical reactions within the cells of your

body keep you alive. Chemical reactions take place when you cook food. Chemical reactions take place when you drive a car or light a fire.

Different types of chemical reactions

Thermal decomposition
Some substances split up when you heat them to form new substances. This type of reaction is called **thermal decomposition**. Examples of this are given below:

$$\text{calcium carbonate} \xrightarrow{\text{HEAT}} \text{calcium oxide} + \text{carbon dioxide}$$

Calcium oxide is also called quick lime and is used in mortar and cement. Carbon dioxide is a gas and can be used to make dry ice.

$$\text{mercury oxide} \xrightarrow{\text{HEAT}} \text{mercury} + \text{oxygen}$$

Mercury is a liquid metal used in thermometers and barometers. Oxygen is the gas we breathe in order to live.

There is no overall change in **mass** when a chemical reaction takes place. This means that in the first chemical reaction, the mass of the calcium carbonate before the reaction is equal to the mass of the calcium oxide plus the mass of the carbon dioxide after the reaction.

Oxidation reactions

Many substances will react with oxygen to produce oxides. These are called **oxidation** reactions. Some examples of this kind of reaction are given below:

$$\text{magnesium} + \text{oxygen} \rightarrow \text{magnesium oxide}$$

This is a very vigorous reaction which gives off a lot of light. The reaction was used by early photographers for flashlights.

$$\text{carbon} + \text{oxygen} \rightarrow \text{carbon dioxide}$$

$$\text{copper} + \text{oxygen} \rightarrow \text{copper oxide}$$

Some oxidation reactions are not useful. For example, iron will react with the oxygen and water in the air producing iron oxide or rust. This kind of chemical change is called **corrosion**.

Figure 2 **This car has been reacting with the air and water around it to produce rust**

This simple experiment shows that both air and water are needed if an object is to rust.

◆ Tube 1 has nails in dry air – the anhydrous calcium chloride absorbs any water from the air.
◆ Tube 2 has nails in water which has been boiled to remove all the air. The layer of oil stops any more air from entering the water.
◆ Tube 3 has nails exposed to both air and water. Only in this tube have the nails rusted.

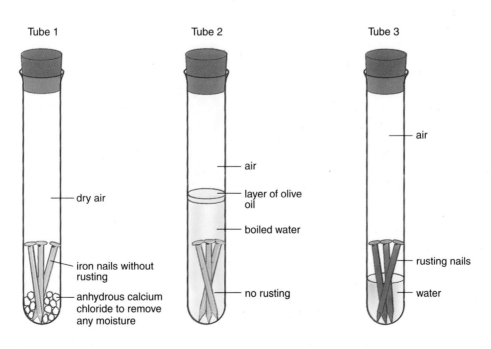

Figure 3 **A demonstration of the conditions needed for rusting to occur**

CHANGING MATERIALS (2)

To stop a surface from corroding it can be coated with paint, grease, plastic or another metal such as tin which does not corrode.

Oxidation of food
Some foods also react with the oxygen in the air. This may affect their taste. There are several ways of trying to avoid this:

◆ food can be vacuum packed so there is no contact between it and the air e.g. bacon
◆ food can be kept in the refrigerator to slow down any reaction that may take place e.g. fats such as lard and butter.

Using chemical reactions to obtain metals
Most metals come from rocks in the ground. Some, such as gold, can be found naturally but most react with other substances in the air or the ground and are found as compounds called **ores**. In order to obtain a metal, the ore needs to be chemically changed.

Getting iron from iron ore
One ore which contains iron is called haematite. It is a compound of iron and oxygen. The oxygen is removed by heating the ore with limestone and coke (carbon) in a blast furnace.

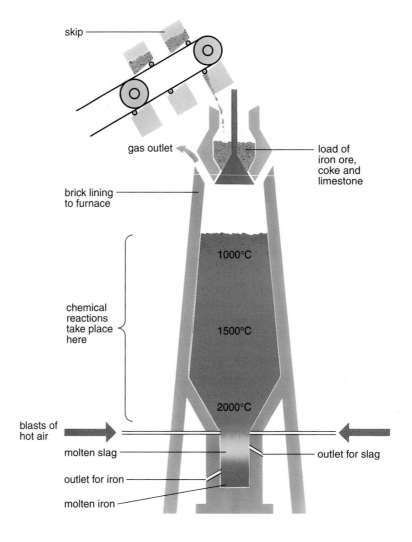

Figure 4 **The blast furnace**

Getting aluminium from aluminium ore

The main ore which contains aluminium is called bauxite. It is a compound of aluminium and oxygen. The two elements are separated by heating the ore until it melts then passing an electric current through it. The process is called **electrolysis**.

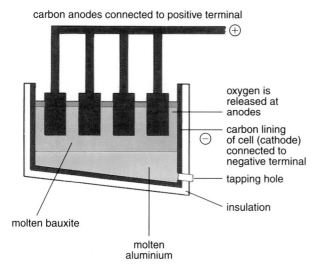

carbon anodes connected to positive terminal

$\oplus$

oxygen is released at anodes

carbon lining of cell (cathode) connected to negative terminal

$\ominus$

tapping hole

insulation

molten bauxite

molten aluminium

Figure 5 **The electrolysis of aluminium ore**

Getting copper from copper ore

There are several ores which contain copper. One of these is copper oxide. The oxygen can be removed from the copper oxide by heating the ore with powdered coke in a furnace.

copper + carbon → copper + carbon
oxide   metal   monoxide

Key terms

Check that you understand and can explain the following terms:

* chemical reaction
* raw material
* chemical change
* thermal decomposition
* mass
* oxidation
* corrosion
* ore
* electrolysis

Questions

1 Write down the name of five objects in your room which have been chemically changed.

2 What are the two main features of a chemical change?

3 Which of the following are chemical changes:

   a) burning a match
   b) mixing cement, sand and water to make concrete
   c) melting a piece of wax
   d) boiling some water?

4 Explain the phrase *thermal decomposition* and give one example of this kind of reaction.

5 Give one example of an oxidation reaction and explain why it is a useful reaction.

6 What conditions are necessary for an iron nail to rust?

7 Suggest three ways in which you might prevent a sheet of iron from corroding.

8 Why are some foods vacuum packed?

9 Why are most metals not found as a pure element in the ground?

10 How do the chemical reactions in a blast furnace chemically change the ore haematite?

7.4 BURNING FUELS

Fuels such as coal, oil, gas and wood are very useful sources of energy. We burn them in order to release the energy they contain. A chemical reaction which releases energy is called an **exothermic reaction**. A chemical reaction which takes in energy is called an **endothermic reaction**.

The energy generated by the burning of fuels can be used to produce electricity, cook food, provide warmth or produce light.

Figure 1 **The energy released when coal is burned at this power station is used to produce electricity**

The above reaction can be described by the word equation.

> **FUEL**   **CARBON DIOXIDE**
> **+**   →   **+**
> **OXYGEN**   **WATER**   **+**   **ENERGY**
> **+**
> **WASTE PRODUCTS**
> **(e.g. ash)**

Although there are many advantages in using these fuels to provide the energy we need, there are also several disadvantages:

1. when fuels are burned they increase the amount of carbon dioxide in the atmosphere. Carbon dioxide is one of the gases which causes **global warming**.

2. other gases, such as sulphur dioxide and nitrogen oxides, are sometimes released into the atmosphere. These gases can cause **acid rain** (see page 94).

The products of a reaction can sometimes be changed by altering the conditions of the reaction.

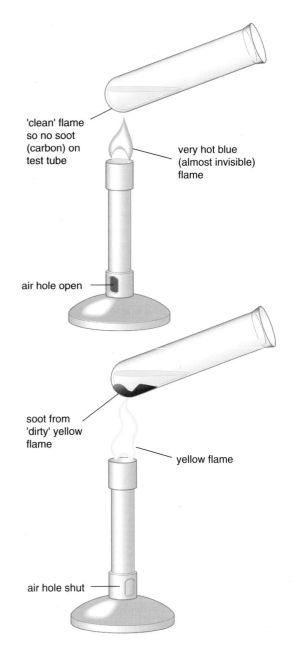

'clean' flame so no soot (carbon) on test tube

very hot blue (almost invisible) flame

air hole open

soot from 'dirty' yellow flame

yellow flame

air hole shut

Figure 2 **The gas does not burn completely when the air hole in the Bunsen burner is closed**

Combustion is another word for burning.

Testing for some of the products of a chemical reaction

Testing for carbon dioxide

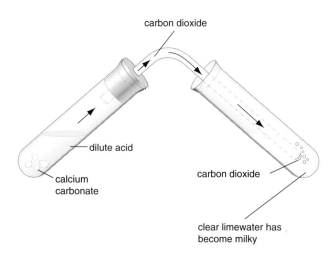

Figure 3 Limewater turns milky if carbon dioxide is bubbled through it for a few minutes

Testing for oxygen

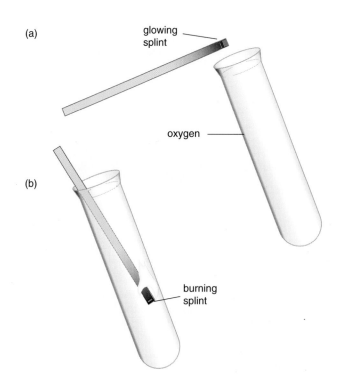

Figure 4 A glowing splint will relight when placed in a test tube filled with oxygen

Key terms

Check that you understand and can explain the following terms:

* fuel
* exothermic reaction
* endothermic reaction
* global warming
* acid rain
* combustion

Questions

1 What is an exothermic reaction?

2 What is an endothermic reaction?

3 Give three possible uses for the energy which is released when a fuel is burned.

4 Give two disadvantages of burning fossil fuels.

5 Why is there incomplete combustion when the air hole of a Bunsen burner is closed?

6 Give two possible advantages of complete combustion over incomplete combustion when using a Bunsen burner.

7 Which gas causes each of these effects:

a) relights a glowing splint
b) burns with a pop
c) turns limewater milky?

Testing for hydrogen

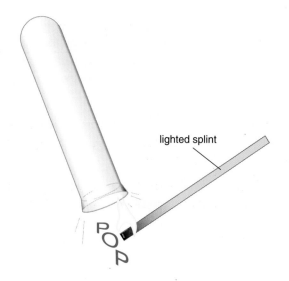

Figure 5 Hydrogen burns with a pop

CHANGING MATERIALS (2)

What you need to know!

1 When a chemical reaction takes place there is no overall change in mass.

2 Many useful materials are made through chemical reactions.

3 Chemical reactions can be described by word equations.

4 There are several different types of chemical reaction including thermal decomposition and oxidation.

5 Metals can be obtained from their oxides (ores).

6 Some oxidation reactions, such as corrosion, are not useful.

7 There are several ways to stop or slow down unwanted oxidation reactions, such as rusting.

8 The energy transfers that accompany chemical reactions can be useful e.g. the burning of fuels.

9 The burning of fossil fuels may damage the environment.

How much do you know?

1 Here is a list of some of the materials which may be used to build a house.

stone	concrete
brick	aluminium
slate	steel
glass	lead
wood	plastic

Complete the table below to show which materials are natural and which have been made or chemically changed. Two spaces have already been filled in for you.

Natural material	Man-made material
wood	lead

8 marks

2 Here are two lists. The first is a list of raw materials, the second is a list of manufactured materials.

Draw a line from each of the raw materials to the manufactured material it can be made into. The first one has been done for you.

sand	bread
iron ore	paper
wood	steel
clay	plastic
flour	glass
oil	brick

5 marks

3 Three shiny iron nails A, B and C are placed in sealed test tubes as shown in the diagrams below.

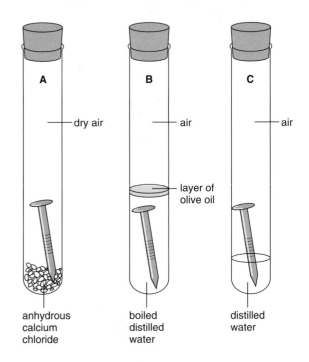

A — dry air
B — air
C — air

layer of olive oil

anhydrous calcium chloride

boiled distilled water

distilled water

a) Which nail will corrode?

_____

1 mark

b) Suggest two ways in which the nail can be treated, before it is put into the test tube, to prevent it from corroding.

_____

_____

2 marks

How much do you know? continued

4 New materials are often made by heating one or more substances so that a chemical reaction takes place.

Tick the three boxes which describe a chemical change.

☐ Heating wax to make it melt
☐ Heating the ingredients of a cake in an oven
☐ Boiling a kettle filled with water
☐ Grilling some bread to make toast
☐ Burning gas on a stove

3 marks

5 The word equation below describes what happens when an oil lamp is lit. Fill in the missing words

OIL + ___ →___ ___ + WATER + HEAT + LIGHT

2 marks

6 Bill collects samples of three different gases in six test tubes. Test tubes A and B contain oxygen, test tubes C and D contain carbon dioxide and test tubes E and F contain hydrogen.

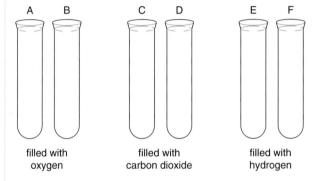

filled with   filled with   filled with
oxygen   carbon dioxide   hydrogen

Bill then:

a) adds a few drops of limewater to test tubes A, C and E
b) inserts a lighted splint into test tubes B, D and F

Fill in the table below, adding rows for tubes B–F, showing what happens in each case. If nothing happens write 'nothing happens'.

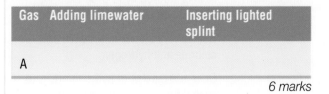

Gas	Adding limewater	Inserting lighted splint
A		

6 marks

7 The diagram below shows two Bunsen burners being used to heat equal amounts of water. One Bunsen burner has its air hole open, the other has its air hole closed.

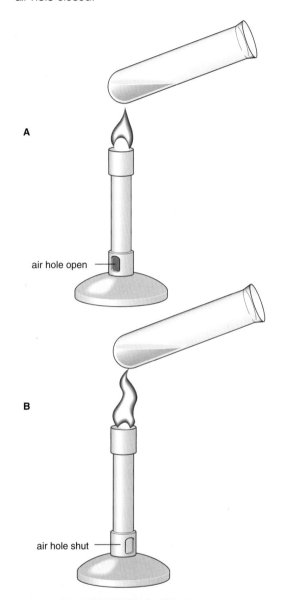

A

air hole open

B

air hole shut

a) Explain why the water being heated by Bunsen burner A will boil first.

_____

_____

2 marks

b) What will happen to the bottom of the test tube being heated by Bunsen burner B?

_____

1 mark

8.1 CHEMICAL REACTIONS AND THE REACTIVITY SERIES

Many metals will react with other substances to form new compounds. By comparing these reactions we can list the metals in order of **reactivity**. This is called the **reactivity series**.

Reactions between metals and oxygen

Most metals will react with oxygen to form a metal oxide.

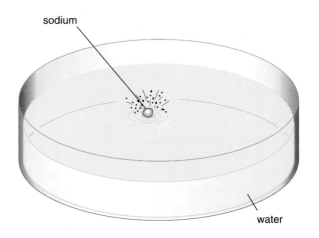

sodium

water

Figure 2 **Reacting a metal with water**

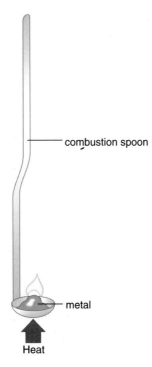

combustion spoon

metal

Heat

Figure 1 **Reacting a metal with oxygen**

Metal	Reaction with oxygen
Sodium	Burns brightly in air to form a white powder, sodium peroxide
Magnesium	Catches fire after being heated and burns with a bright white flame. A white powder, magnesium oxide, is formed by the reaction
Iron filings	Do not burn but glow brightly if heated strongly. They react with the oxygen to form black iron oxide
Copper foil	Does not burn but if it is heated strongly a coating of black copper oxide forms

Reactions between metals and water

Many metals will react with water to form a metal oxide or hydroxide.

Metal	Reaction with water
Sodium	Reacts violently with cold water becoming so hot that it melts and whizzes around on a layer of hydrogen
Magnesium	Reacts very slowly with cold water forming magnesium hydroxide and hydrogen
Iron	Reacts extremely slowly with cold water (days or weeks) to produce iron oxide and hydrogen
Copper	Does not react with water so it is often used for water pipes

Reactions between metals and an acid (hydrochloric acid)

Metal	Reaction with acid
Sodium	The reaction between dilute hydrochloric acid and sodium is extremely violent and is too dangerous to carry out
Magnesium	Reacts vigorously to produce magnesium chloride and hydrogen
Iron	Reacts very slowly to produce iron chloride and hydrogen
Copper	Does not react with hydrochloric acid even if the acid is concentrated

Experiments like those given previously can be used to compile a reactivity series for metals. This is given below:

Potassium (K)
Sodium (Na)
Calcium (Ca)
Magnesium (Mg)
Aluminium (Al)
Zinc (Zn)
Iron (Fe)
Lead (Pb)
Copper (Cu)
Silver (Ag)
Gold (Au)

Most reactive metals

Least reactive metals

This sentence might help you to remember the order of the metals in the series:

Poor **S**ally **C**an't **M**anage **A**ny **Z**eal **I**n **L**atin **C**os **S**he's **G**lum

The more reactive a metal is, the more it *wants* to form compounds. We can use this idea to predict what will happen in a **displacement reaction**.

Displacement reactions

In a displacement reaction a more reactive metal will displace a less reactive metal from a salt solution.

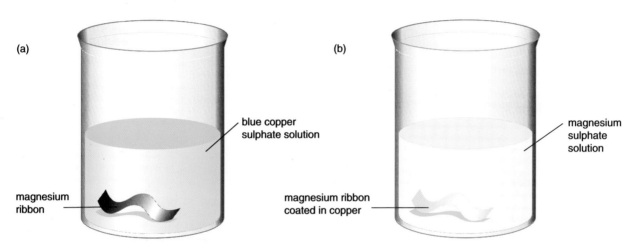

(a) blue copper sulphate solution

magnesium ribbon

(b) magnesium sulphate solution

magnesium ribbon coated in copper

Figure 3 **The displacement of copper by magnesium**

This reaction is described by the equation:

magnesium + copper → magnesium + copper
         sulphate   sulphate

The **more reactive** magnesium goes into solution and displaces the **less reactive** copper. The copper is forced out of solution and forms a coating on the magnesium ribbon.

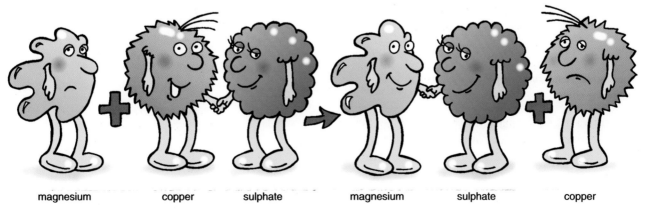

magnesium   copper   sulphate   magnesium   sulphate   copper

Figure 4

PATTERNS OF BEHAVIOUR

A different displacement reaction takes place if copper metal is added to a silver salt solution.

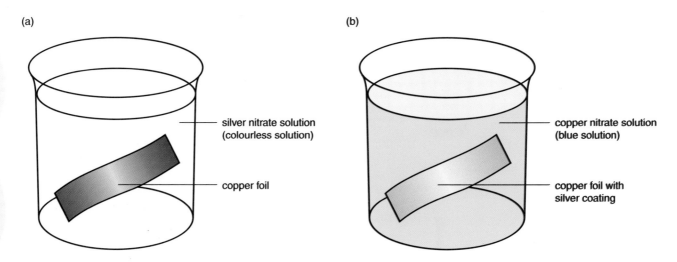

(a)

silver nitrate solution (colourless solution)

copper foil

(b)

copper nitrate solution (blue solution)

copper foil with silver coating

Figure 5 **The displacement of silver by copper**

This reaction is described by the equation:

copper + silver nitrate → copper nitrate + silver

copper   silver   nitrate   copper   nitrate   silver

Figure 6

The **more reactive** copper displaces the **less reactive** silver.

Competing for oxygen

If a mixture of iron powder and copper oxide is heated, a displacement reaction takes place. The iron displaces the copper because it is higher in the reactivity series.

iron + copper oxide → iron oxide + copper

iron   copper   oxide

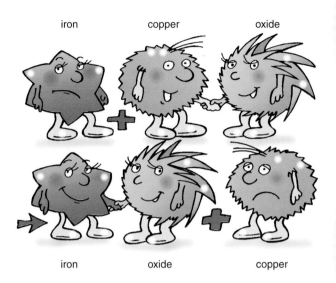

iron   oxide   copper

Figure 7 **The displacement of copper by iron**

The **more reactive** iron displaces the **less reactive** copper.

If a mixture of aluminium powder and iron oxide is heated, a displacement reaction takes place. The aluminium displaces the iron because it is higher in the reactivity series.

aluminium + iron oxide $\rightarrow$ aluminium oxide + iron

aluminium   iron   oxide

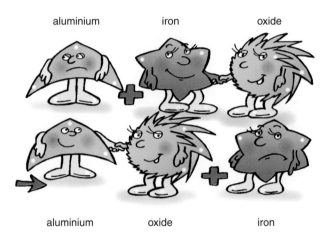

aluminium   oxide   iron

Figure 8 **The displacement of iron by aluminium**

The **more reactive** aluminium displaces the **less reactive** iron.

Both of these reactions give out heat when they take place. They are **exothermic** reactions.

Key terms

Check that you understand and can explain the following terms:

- ★ reactivity
- ★ reactivity series
- ★ displacement reaction
- ★ more reactive
- ★ less reactive
- ★ exothermic reaction

Questions

1 Name one metal which will not react with oxygen even when heated.

2 Name a metal whose reaction with water is more violent than that between sodium and water.

3 Name a metal which, when added to hydrochloric acid, reacts more vigorously than iron but less vigorously than calcium.

4 Explain what is meant by the reactivity series.

5 What is a displacement reaction? Give two examples of a displacement reaction and write a word equation for each.

PATTERNS OF BEHAVIOUR

ACIDS, ALKALIS AND BASES

Acids

All the objects in this photograph contain **acid**.

Figure 1

In everyday life there are acids all around us. They are found not only in chemical laboratories and factories but also in our homes and even inside our bodies. The sharp taste of a lemon is caused by citric acid. The taste of sour milk is caused by lactic acid. A car battery contains sulphuric acid. Our stomachs contain hydrochloric acid to help us digest our food.

Bases and alkalis

All the objects in this photograph contain **bases** or **alkalis**. An alkali is a base which will dissolve in water.

Figure 2

Bases are the chemical opposites of acids. They are **antacids** and can be used to **neutralise** the effect of acids. For example, if you eat too many green apples you may have indigestion or stomach ache. This happens because there is too much acid in your stomach. To neutralise the effects of the excess acid and so stop the discomfort you may take some indigestion tablets or stomach powders which contain bases.

The sting of a wasp is alkaline so the discomfort it causes can be neutralised by vinegar which is acidic. The sting of a bee is acidic so the discomfort it causes can be neutralised using an antacid.

Figure 3 Most crops grow best if the soil in which they are planted is very slightly acidic. If the soil becomes too acidic, however, growth is poor. To prevent this, a base (lime) is added

Reactions between acids and bases/alkalis

The reaction between an acid and a base or alkali can be described by the equation:

ACID + BASE or ALKALI → SALT + WATER

Examples

hydrochloric acid + sodium hydroxide → sodium chloride + water
(acid)   (alkali)   (salt)

nitric acid + potassium hydroxide → potassium nitrate + water
(acid)   (alkali)   (salt)

sulphuric acid + magnesium oxide → magnesium sulphate + water
(acid)   (base)   (salt)

Sodium chloride, potassium nitrate and magnesium sulphate are all examples of **salts**.

◆ Salts made from hydrochloric acid are called chlorides.
◆ Salts made from nitric acid are called nitrates.
◆ Salts made from sulphuric acid are called sulphates.

Reactions between acids and metals

Acids can be highly corrosive. They will react with both metals and non-metals.

The reaction between an acid and a metal can described by the equation:

ACID + METAL → SALT + HYDROGEN

Examples

hydrochloric acid + magnesium → magnesium chloride + hydrogen
(acid)   (metal)   (salt)

sulphuric acid + calcium → calcium sulphate + hydrogen
(acid)   (metal)   (salt)

nitric acid + potassium → potassium nitrate + hydrogen
(acid)   (metal)   (salt)

Reactions between acids and carbonates

The reaction between an acid and a carbonate can be described by the equation:

ACID + CARBONATE → SALT + CARBON DIOXIDE + WATER

Examples

hydrochloric acid + magnesium carbonate → magnesium chloride + carbon dioxide + water

sulphuric acid + calcium carbonate → calcium sulphate + carbon dioxide + water

nitric acid + potassium carbonate → potassium nitrate + carbon dioxide + water

Acid rain

Metals, rocks, buildings and statues often suffer from the corrosive effects of **acid rain**. This is formed when gases such as carbon dioxide, sulphur dioxide and nitrogen dioxide dissolve in rain water. These gases are released into the atmosphere by cars, lorries, factories and power stations.

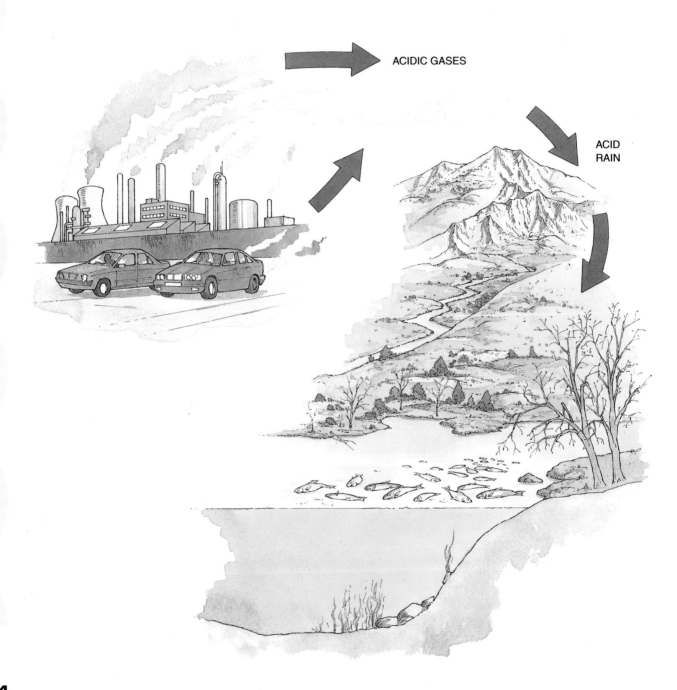

ACIDIC GASES

ACID RAIN

Figure 4 **The formation of acid rain**

As acid rain runs down the hills it can affect the chemistry of the soil, killing trees and plants. When the acid rain reaches ponds and lakes it makes them acidic, killing many of the creatures that live in the water. Acid rain can also eat away the surfaces of statues and buildings.

It is very important that industry and car owners reduce the amounts of these chemicals being released into the atmosphere.

Indicators

Some dyes, such as **litmus**, are different colours in acid or alkaline solution. In an acid solution litmus is red, but in an alkaline solution it is blue. A dye which changes colour in this way is called an **indicator**.

One of the most useful indicators is **universal indicator**. This is a mixture of dyes and can produce a range of colours. Its colour indicates the strength of an acid or alkali.

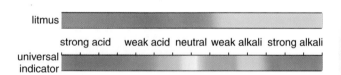

Figure 5 **The colours of litmus and universal indicator with solutions of different pH**

The pH scale

Scientists also use a numbered scale, known as the **pH scale**, to describe the acidity of solutions.

◆ A neutral solution has a pH value of 7.
◆ Solutions which are acidic have a pH value less than 7.
◆ Solutions which are alkaline have a pH value higher than 7 (up to a maximum of pH 14).

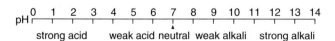

Figure 6 **The pH scale**

Key terms

Check that you understand and can explain the following terms:

★ acid (ic)   ★ acid rain
★ base   ★ litmus
★ alkali (ne)   ★ indicator
★ antacid   ★ universal indicator
★ neutralise   ★ pH scale
★ salt

Questions

1 Give two examples of everyday materials which a) contain acid and b) contain alkali.

2 Explain why indigestion powder eases the pain you might experience if you eat too many unripe, green apples.

3 Explain why the discomfort caused by a wasp sting can be eased by rubbing vinegar onto the sting.

4 What is produced when
   a) an acid and a metal react together
   b) an acid and an alkali react together
   c) an acid and a carbonate react together?

5 How is acid rain formed?

6 Give two examples of the damage caused by acid rain.

7 How can the damage caused by acid rain be reduced?

8 What is an indicator used for?

9 What pH should soil have to grow healthy crops?

10 Match the descriptions of the solutions in the first column with their pH values.

Neutral solution	pH 6
Slightly alkaline	pH 1
Very acidic	pH 7
Slightly acidic	pH 14
Very alkaline	pH 8

What you need to know!

1 Most metals will react with other substances such as oxygen, water and acid.

2 Some metals are more reactive than others.

3 By observing their reactions, metals can be placed in a reactivity series.

4 It is possible to predict how metals will react if their position in the reactivity series is known.

5 Displacement reactions may take place between metals and solutions of other metals.

6 Acids will react with most metals and bases to form salts.

7 It is possible to neutralise the effects of acids and alkalis using antacids and acids, respectively.

8 Acid rain is caused by sulphur dioxide, carbon dioxide and nitrogen dioxide dissolving in rain water.

9 Acid rain can kill plants and fish. It can also corrode metal, rock and stone.

10 Indicators can be used to discover whether a solution is acidic, neutral or alkaline.

11 The pH scale measures the acidity of a solution.

How much do you know?

1 The diagram below shows four test tubes containing equal amounts of a metal powder and 20cm³ of dilute hydrochloric acid. The number of bubbles of hydrogen being given off indicates the speed of the reaction.

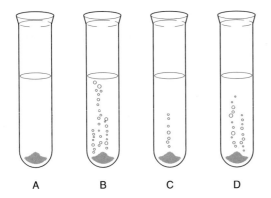

A   B   C   D

Place the four metals in order of reactivity.

Most reactive   _____

_____

_____

Least reactive   _____

4 marks

2 The list below shows four metals in order of their reactivity.

Most reactive   sodium
                     calcium
                     magnesium
Least reactive   copper

a) Using the above information complete the table opposite.

Metal	What happened when added to water
Sodium	Violent reaction, lots of bubbles of gas released
Calcium	
Magnesium	Very slow reaction with cold water, very few bubbles
Copper	

2 marks

b) Name the gas released when sodium reacts with water?

_____

1 mark

c) Why are copper pipes used in houses to carry water?

_____

1 mark

d) Name the gas released when sulphuric acid reacts with calcium carbonate.

_____

1 mark

e) Name the salt produced when sulphuric acid reacts with calcium carbonate.

_____

1 marks

How much do you know? continued

3 An iron nail is placed in a solution of copper sulphate. After 24 hrs it is found that the nail is coated with a reddish-brown material.

a) What is the reddish-brown coating on the nail?

_____

1 mark

b) What kind of reaction has taken place?

_____

1 mark

c) Write a word equation which describes this reaction.

_____

4 marks

d) Which is higher in the reactivity series, iron or copper?

_____

1 mark

4 The chart below shows the pH of several household substances.

Substance	pH
Vinegar	2.9
Fresh milk	6.8
Oven spray	12.5
Brasso	9.5
Jif	11.0

a) Which substance is very alkaline?

_____

1 mark

b) Which substance is very acidic?

_____

1 mark

c) Which substance is almost neutral?

_____

1 mark

d) A wasp sting is slightly alkaline. Which of the substances in the chart could best be used to neutralise a wasp sting?

_____

1 mark

5 The table below shows the colours of two indicators in solutions of different acidity

pH	1	5	7	9	14
Methyl orange	Red		Orange		Yellow
Litmus	Red		Purple		Blue

a) What colour is litmus when added to a neutral solution?

_____

1 mark

b) What colour is methyl orange when added to an acidic solution?

_____

1 mark

c) To what type of solution must litmus be added for it to turn blue?

_____

1 mark

d) What is the pH value of pure distilled water?

_____

1 mark

9.1 STATIC ELECTRICITY

Figure 1 **This spectacular flash of lightning is caused by** static electricity

Static electricity

All objects are made from very small particles called **atoms**. Inside these atoms are even smaller particles called **protons**, **neutrons** and **electrons**. Protons are in the centre of an atom and have a **positive charge**. Neutrons are in the centre of an atom and have no charge. Electrons orbit the centre of an atom and have a **negative charge**.

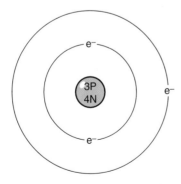

Figure 2 **A neutral atom**

Normally the numbers of protons and electrons in an atom are equal so the atom is **neutral** i.e. has no net charge. It is possible to alter this balance of charges by rubbing two **insulators**, such as a piece of plastic and a cloth, together. An insulator is a material which

does not allow charges to flow through it (see page 102). The rod steals electrons from the cloth and becomes negatively charged. The cloth now has too few electrons and so is positively charged.

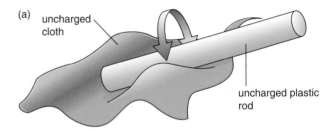

Figure 3a) **The neutral cloth and rod are rubbed together**

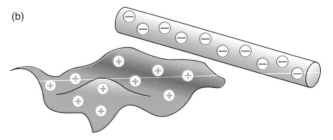

b) **After rubbing, the rod is negatively charged because it has too many electrons and the cloth is positively charged because it has too few electrons**

Attraction and repulsion between charges

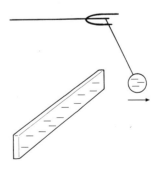

Figure 4a) **If two** like-charged **objects are placed near each other they** repel

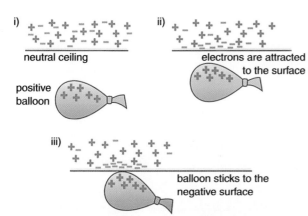

b) **If two** oppositely-charged **objects are placed near each other they** attract

More examples of static electricity

A balloon can be charged by rubbing it on a piece of cloth. If it is then placed against a wall it will often stick to it. This happens because of static electricity.

The negatively-charged balloon repels some of the negative charges in the wall. The surface of the wall therefore becomes positively charged. As opposite charges attract, the negatively-charged balloon sticks to the wall.

i)

neutral ceiling

positive balloon

ii)

electrons are attracted to the surface

iii)

balloon sticks to the negative surface

Figure 5 **A demonstration of static electricity**

Key terms

Check that you understand and can explain the following terms:

* static electricity
* atom
* proton
* neutron
* electron
* positive charge
* negative charge
* neutral
* insulator
* like charges
* repel
* opposite charges
* attract

Questions

1 A neutral object contains equal numbers of _____ and _____.

2 Like charges _____. Opposite charges _____.

3 Which particle inside an atom has a) a positive charge, b) a negative charge and c) no charge?

4 What is an insulator? Name three materials that are insulators.

5 Explain how static electricity can be produced by rubbing two insulators together.

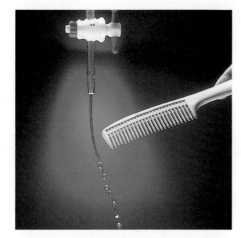

Figure 6 **Water is pulled towards a positively-charged comb which is held close by**

In a similar way, a stream of water will be attracted to a charged plastic comb held close to it. A comb which has just been used is also able to pick up small pieces of paper.

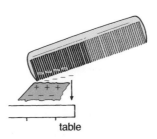

table

Figure 7 **The positively-charged comb is able to attract a small piece of paper**

ELECTRICITY

Making charges move

A **cell** is a kind of pump which makes charges move. This *flow* of charge is called an **electric current**. If a large current is needed, a more powerful pump can be used. The push of a cell is measured in **volts** (V).

The push given to charges can also be increased by connecting two or more cells together. Several cells connected together are called a **battery**. When the cells are connected together it is important that they are all pushing in the same direction.

Simple circuits

Just like water flowing through pipes, charges need something to travel through. The 'pipes' for charges are metal wires. The wires, batteries and bulbs form **circuits** around which currents flow. Figure 1 shows a **complete circuit** as the charges can flow all the way around. When current is flowing, the bulb glows.

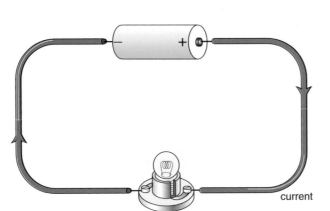

current

Figure 1 **A complete circuit**

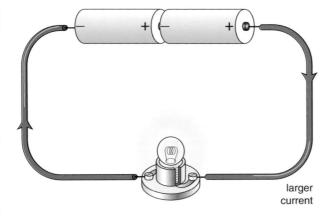

larger current

Figure 2 **A complete two cell circuit**

If one of the wires is removed, current will stop flowing and the bulb will go out. Current will not flow if the circuit is **incomplete**.

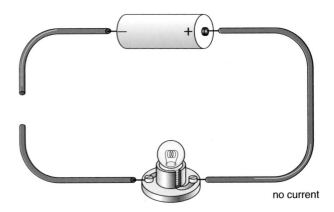

no current

Figure 3 **An incomplete circuit**

The position of the break in the circuit is unimportant. *Current will only flow if the circuit is complete.*

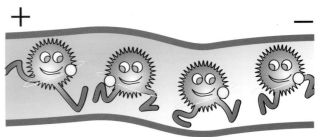

Complete circuit

Incomplete circuit

Figure 4

Circuit diagrams

Drawing diagrams such as those shown opposite is not easy. To simplify things scientists and electricians use **circuit diagrams**. These simple diagrams use symbols to represent the various bits and pieces (more properly called **components**) of the circuit.

(a)

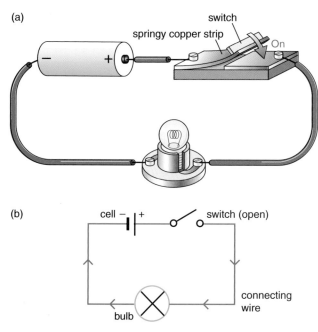

(b)

Figure 5a) **Actual circuit and** b) **circuit diagram of the same circuit**

A list of some of the most common components is shown here.

What it is	What it looks like	Symbol	What it does
Cell			Pulls and pushes charges around a circuit.
Battery			Provides a larger current than a single cell.
Connecting wire			Provides a path through which current can flow.
Lamp/bulb			Glow brightly if sufficient current flows through it.
Switch			Turns current in a circuit on or off.
Resistor			Reduces the current flowing in a circuit
Variable resistor			By altering the value of a variable resistor the size of the current can be changed.

Key terms

Check that you understand and can explain the following terms:

★ cell
★ electric current
★ volts
★ battery
★ circuit
★ complete circuit
★ incomplete circuit
★ circuit diagram
★ components

Questions

1 What is the main use of a cell in a simple circuit?

2 What do we call two or more cells connected together? Explain why two cells might be connected together.

3 What is an electric current?

4 What is a) a complete circuit and b) an incomplete circuit?

5 Draw the symbol for

a) a switch, b) a bulb, c) a battery.

9.3 CONTROLLING CURRENT

In most circuits the negative charges (the electrons) are made to move by a cell or battery. Electronic and electrical devices, such as radios, calculators and televisions, contain components which control the movement of these electrons and make them do something useful.

Switches

A **switch** turns a circuit on and off. It behaves like a drawbridge which can make the circuit complete when closed or incomplete when open.

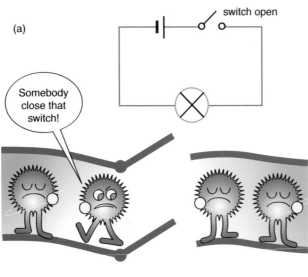

(a)

switch open

Somebody close that switch!

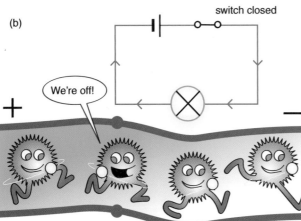

(b)

switch closed

We're off!

+   −

Figure 1a) **When the switch is open, the circuit is incomplete and the current cannot flow**
b) **When the switch is closed, the circuit is complete and the current can flow**

Conductors and insulators

At present, no current can flow around this circuit (Figure 2) because it is incomplete.

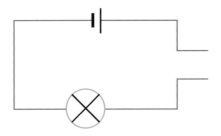

Figure 2 **An incomplete circuit**

If a material which allows electricity to flow through it, i.e. a **conductor**, is placed across the gap, the circuit is complete and so the bulb glows. If a material which does not allow electricity to flow through it, i.e. an **insulator**, is placed across the gap, the circuit is still incomplete and so the bulb does not glow.

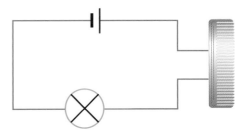

Figure 3a) **An insulator will not allow electricity to flow through it**

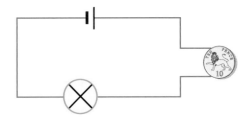

b) **A conductor will allow electricity to flow through it**

Current and resistance

When the switch in this circuit is closed, there is a good flow of charge through the bulb so it glows brightly.

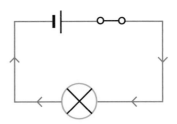

Figure 4a) **The current is large when there is little or no resistance in the circuit**

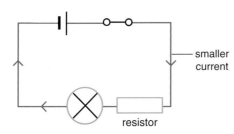

b) **The current is smaller if a resistor is included in the circuit**

When a **resistor** is put into the circuit, the bulb becomes dimmer showing that the rate of flow of charge, i.e. the current, has decreased.

The effect of connecting a resistor into a circuit can be explained by picturing the charges as runners on an athletics track and the resistor as an obstacle such as set of step ladders. Without the resistor, the charges flow freely around the track. When the resistor is put into the circuit, a bottleneck is produced which reduces the flow.

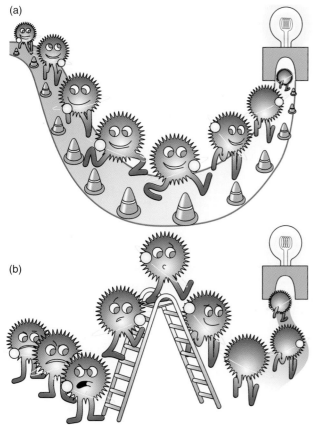

Figure 5 We could imagine a resistor as being an obstacle such as a ladder

Resistors have values measured in **ohms**. The larger the value of the resistor, the greater the obstacle for the charges and the smaller the current in the circuit.

Key terms

Check that you understand and can explain the following terms:

* switch
* conductor
* insulator
* resistor
* ohms
* variable resistor

Questions

1 What is the main use of a switch in a circuit?

2 What is an insulator? Give three examples of materials that are insulators.

3 What is a conductor? Give three examples of materials that are conductors.

4 Give four examples of circuits in the home that contain variable resistors.

If a **variable resistor** is included in a circuit, its value can be altered to increase or decrease the current. Variable resistors are used to control the loudness of the music from a stereo system and the colour and brightness of the picture on a TV set.

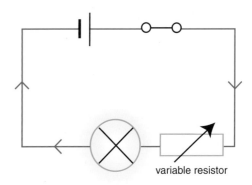

Figure 6 By altering the value of the variable resistor, the bulb can be made to glow more or less brightly

ELECTRICITY

Series and parallel circuits

There are two kinds of electrical circuits – **series** and **parallel**.

A **series circuit** is one in which the electrons have no choice as to which path to follow, i.e. there are no branches in the circuit.

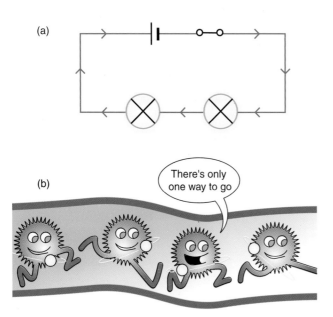

Figure 1 **A series circuit**

In a series circuit the same current passes through all the bulbs. If one of the bulbs is turned off, they are all turned off.

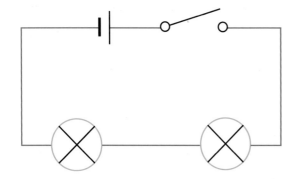

Figure 2

A **parallel circuit** is one in which the electrons do have a choice as to which path they follow.

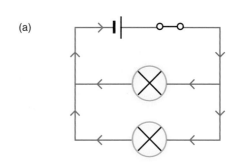

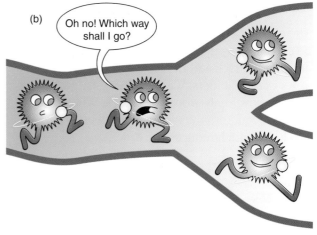

Figure 3 **A parallel circuit**

In a parallel circuit it is possible to switch off some of the bulbs and yet leave others on.

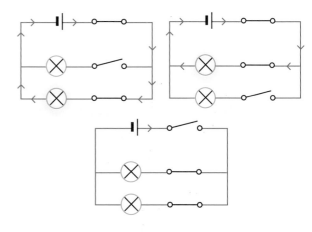

Figure 4

Measuring current

The size of a current is measured using an instrument called an **ammeter**. The ammeter is placed **in series** with the part of the circuit being investigated.

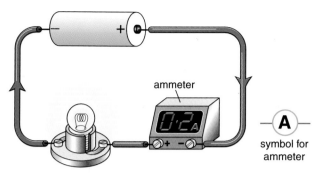

Figure 5 **Using an ammeter to measure the current**

symbol for ammeter

Currents in series circuits

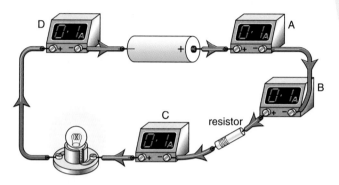

Figure 6 **Measuring current in a series circuit**

◆ Ammeter A is measuring how much current is leaving the cell.
◆ Ammeter B is reading how much current is flowing into the resistor.
◆ Ammeter C is reading how much current is flowing into the bulb.
◆ Ammeter D is reading how much current is flowing back into the cell.

From these readings it is clear that

1 the current leaving the cell is the same size as the current returning to it. Current is not 'used up' as it flows around a circuit.
2 the size of the current is the same in all parts of a series circuit.

Key terms

Check that you understand and can explain the following terms:

★ series circuit ★ in series
★ parallel circuit ★ ammeter

Questions

1 Draw a series circuit which contains a battery, four bulbs and a switch. What happens when the switch is opened and closed?

2 Draw a parallel circuit which contains a cell, four bulbs and two switches. The switches are connected so that one switch turns two bulbs on and off whilst the second turns all four bulbs on and off.

3 Redraw the circuit for Question 2 but include two ammeters to measure the currents leaving and returning to the cell.

Currents in parallel circuits

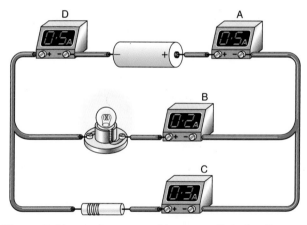

Figure 7 **Measuring current in a parallel circuit**

◆ Ammeter A is measuring how much current is leaving the cell.
◆ Ammeter B is reading how much current is flowing through the bulb.
◆ Ammeter C is reading how much current is flowing through the resistor.
◆ Ammeter D is reading how much current is flowing back into the cell.

From these readings it is clear that

1 the size of the current in the different parts of a parallel circuit is not the same.
2 the current leaving the cell is the same size as the current returning to it.

ELECTRICITY

What you need to know!

1 There are two types of charges – positive charges and negative charges.

2 These charges can be produced by rubbing two insulators together.

3 Like charges repel while opposite charges attract.

4 Uncharged objects have equal numbers of positive and negative charges.

5 An electric current is a flow or movement of charge.

6 A switch turns a circuit on or off by making it complete or incomplete.

How much do you know?

1 The diagrams below are of five objects made from five different materials.

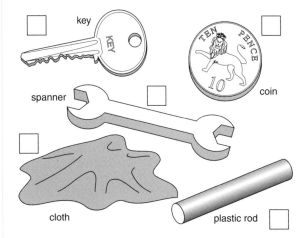

key
coin
spanner
cloth
plastic rod

Which two will produce static electricity when rubbed together? Tick the appropriate boxes.

2 marks

2 The diagrams below are of three pairs of balloons.

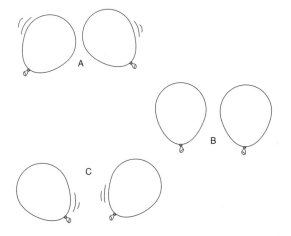

A

B

C

a)   Which pair of balloons have like charges?

_____

1 mark

b)   Which pair of balloons have opposite charges?

_____

1 mark

c)   Which pair of balloons are uncharged?

_____

1 mark

3 When a balloon is rubbed on John's jumper it becomes positively charged.

a)   What charge does John's jumper have?

_____

1 mark

b)   Explain how the balloon has become positively charged.

_____

_____

_____

_____

2 marks

4 Katy built the circuit shown below.

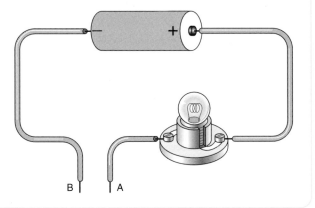

B   A

How much do you know? continued

a) Why did the bulb not glow?

_____

1 mark

b) Katy placed each of the objects below in turn, across the gap AB.

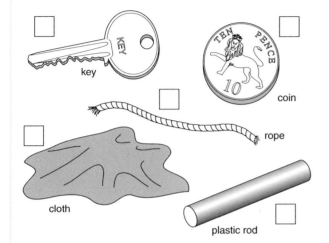

key

coin

rope

cloth

plastic rod

Which two objects made the bulb glow? Tick the appropriate boxes.

2 marks

c) Why did the bulb glow when either of these two objects was placed across the gap AB?

_____

_____

2 marks

a) In which circuit will the bulb(s) glow the brightest?

_____

1 mark

b) In which circuit will the bulb(s) glow least?

_____

1 mark

c) In which two circuits will the bulbs have the same brightness?

_____

2 marks

6 The diagram below shows two similar circuits.

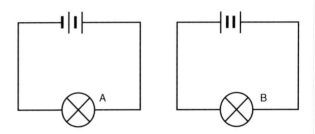

A

B

Explain why bulb A glows but bulb B does not glow.

_____

_____

2 marks

5 In the circuits shown here all the cells and all the bulbs are identical.

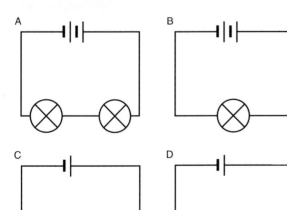

A

B

C

D

7 The diagram below shows an incomplete circuit.

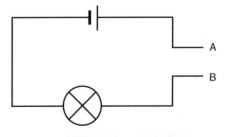

A

B

Explain why the bulb glows brightly when a piece of copper wire is placed across the gap AB but glows dimly if a resistor is placed between A and B.

_____

_____

2 marks

9.5 MAGNETS AND MAGNETISM

Magnetic materials

Figure 1 **Magnetic materials**

Magnets are able to attract objects which are made from certain materials, e.g. iron, steel, nickel and cobalt. These are called **magnetic materials**.

Non-magnetic materials

pieces of paper

Figure 2 **Non-magnetic materials**

Magnets are unable to attract objects which are made from materials such as paper, plastic and copper. These are called **non-magnetic materials**.

Poles of a magnet

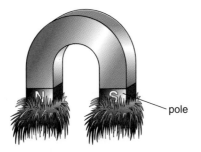

pole

Figure 3 **The magnet is strongest at the poles**

If iron filings are sprinkled over a bar magnet or a horseshoe magnet, most of them will stick to the two ends. These are the strongest parts of the magnets and are called the **poles**. Magnets have two poles, a **north pole** and a **south pole**.

Simple compass

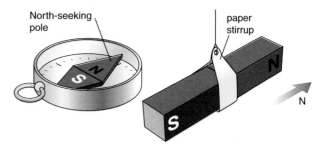

North-seeking pole

paper stirrup

Figure 4 **Using a magnet as a simple compass**

If a bar magnet is suspended so that it is free to rotate, it will eventually come to rest with its north pole pointing northwards and its south pole pointing southwards. The magnet is therefore behaving like a simple **compass**.

Attraction and repulsion between poles

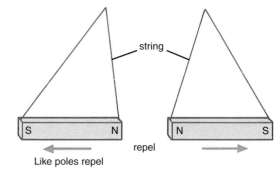

string

repel

Like poles repel

Figure 5 **Repulsion between like poles**

If two similar poles are placed close together they **repel**.

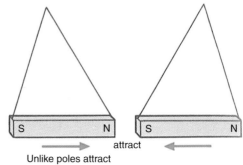

attract

Unlike poles attract

Figure 6 **Attraction between opposite poles**

If two opposite poles are placed close together they **attract**.

Magnetic fields

When an object made of iron or steel is placed close to a magnet, it is attracted towards it. This happens because the object is inside the magnet's **magnetic field**.

Discovering the shape of a magnetic field

1 Using iron filings

A piece of paper is placed over the magnet. Iron filings are gently sprinkled over the paper. The pattern formed by the filings shows the shape of the magnetic field.

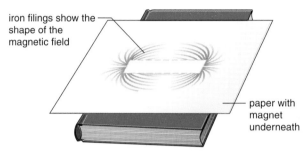

iron filings show the shape of the magnetic field

paper with magnet underneath

Figure 7 **Using iron filings to discover the shape of the magnetic field around a bar magnet**

2 Using a compass

A magnet is placed on top of a piece of paper and drawn around. A compass is placed next to the magnet, a circle drawn around it and the direction of the compass needle marked inside the circle. The compass is then moved so that its tail is next to the compass point just drawn. A circle is again drawn around the compass and its direction recorded. This process is repeated all over the paper. The compass needles on the paper will show the shape of the magnetic field.

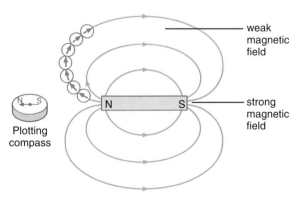

weak magnetic field

strong magnetic field

N   S

Plotting compass

Figure 8 **Using a compass to discover the shape of the magnetic field around a bar magnet**

Key terms

Check that you understand and can explain the following terms:

* ★ magnetic material
* ★ non-magnetic material
* ★ pole
* ★ north pole
* ★ south pole
* ★ compass
* ★ repel
* ★ attract
* ★ magnetic field

Questions

1 Name three magnetic materials.

2 Name three non-magnetic materials.

3 What are the strongest parts of a magnet called?

4 What happens when a) two similar poles are placed next to each other, b) two dissimilar poles are placed next to each other?

5 Draw a diagram showing the field pattern around a bar magnet. Show on your diagram where the field is strongest.

Magnetic field pattern around a bar magnet

Both methods show that the field pattern around a bar magnet is as given in Figure 9.

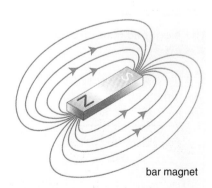

bar magnet

Figure 9 **The shape of the magnetic field around a bar magnet**

Where the field is strong, the lines are drawn close together. Where the field is weak, the lines are drawn well apart.

ELECTROMAGNETISM

When a current flows through a wire, a circular magnetic field is created around it. This field can be seen using either iron filings or compasses.

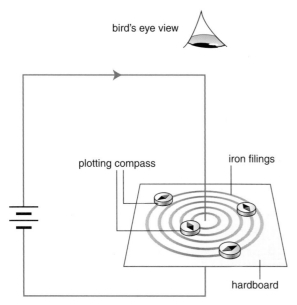

Figure 1 The magnetic field around a current-carrying wire

The field only exists when the current is flowing. If it is turned off, the field disappears.

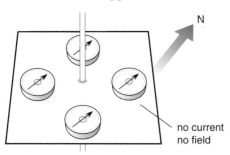

Figure 2 The magnetic field disappears when the current is off

If the current flows in the opposite direction, the field changes direction.

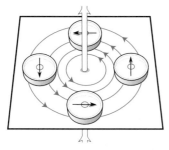

Figure 3 The direction of the magnetic field depends upon the direction of the current

Field strength

The field created when a current flows in a single piece of wire can be quite weak, but its strength can be increased by

◆ increasing the current through the wire
◆ increasing the number of pieces of wire, i.e. making the wire into a coil.

Field shape

The magnetic field around a long coil is the same shape as that around a bar magnet.

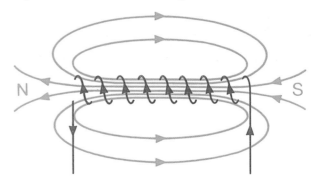

Figure 4 The shape of the magnetic field around a long coil

Electromagnets

An **electromagnet** is made by placing a piece of iron through the centre of a coil. When the current flows around the coil the iron becomes magnetised. When current stops flowing the iron loses its magnetism.

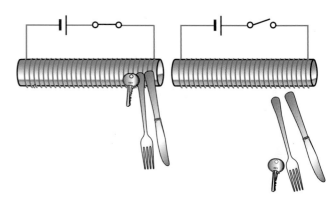

Figure 5 The iron becomes magnetised when the current flows

Electromagnets are very useful because

◆ they can be turned on and off
◆ they can be made stronger and weaker.

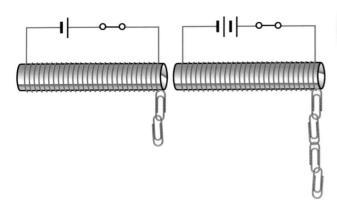

Figure 6 **The strength of the electromagnet depends on the size of the current**

Key terms

Check that you understand and can explain the following terms:

★ electromagnetism
★ field strength
★ electromagnet
★ relay switch
★ iron armature

Questions

1 Draw a diagram of the field pattern around a piece of wire through which a current is flowing.

2 Draw a diagram of the field pattern around a coil through which a current is flowing.

3 How can the field around a coil be made stronger?

4 How might an electromagnet be used to move cars in a scrapyard?

5 Draw a diagram of an electric bell and in your own words, explain how it works.

When the current is small the field is weak.

When the current is larger the field is stronger.

The electric bell

When the button is pressed, current flows around the circuit and the electromagnet at E becomes magnetised. The iron rod is attracted towards it and the hammer hits the bell. While this is happening, a gap appears at the contact screw. The circuit is now incomplete, the electromagnet loses its magnetism and the spring pulls the rod back to its original position. The whole process then begins again. The bell continues to ring as long as the button is pressed.

The relay switch

Sometimes it is useful to be able to control the current flowing in one circuit by using a second circuit. This is especially true if the current flowing in the first circuit is large. This can be done by using a **relay switch**.

In Figure 8, when switch A is closed, the iron core becomes magnetised and attracts the **iron armature**. As the end of the armature (B) is attracted, its other end pushes the wires at C together, turning the second circuit on.

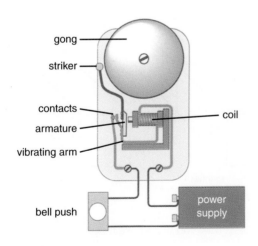

Figure 7 **The electric bell**

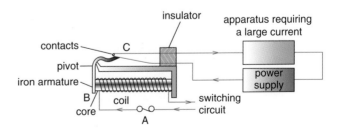

Figure 8 **The relay switch**

If switch A is opened, the electromagnet loses its magnetism, the armature returns to its original position and the second circuit is turned off.

What you need to know!

1   There are two types of electrical circuits – series circuits and parallel circuits.

2   The size of an electric current depends upon the components in the circuit.

3   The size of an electric current is measured in amperes or amps (A).

4   The size of an electric current is measured using an instrument called an ammeter.

5   A magnetic material is attracted to a magnet.

6   A non-magnetic material is not attracted to a magnet.

7   The strongest parts of a magnet are its poles.

8   Similar poles attract. Opposite poles repel.

9   There is a magnetic field around a magnet.

10 A current flowing through a wire produces a magnetic field.

11 An electromagnet can be made by wrapping a length of current-carrying wire around a magnetic material such as iron.

12 Devices such as electric bells, circuit breakers and relay switches contain electromagnets.

How much do you know?

1   Jill built the electrical circuits shown below

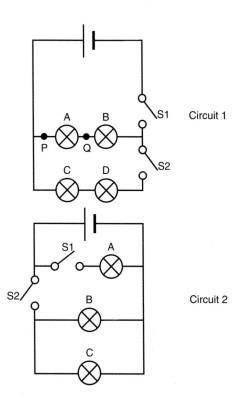

Circuit 1

Circuit 2

c)   In circuit 1 bulb A stops glowing if a piece of wire is connected from P to Q. Explain why this happens.

_____

_____

_____

2 marks

2   The diagram below shows two bar magnets.

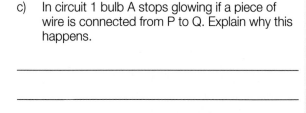

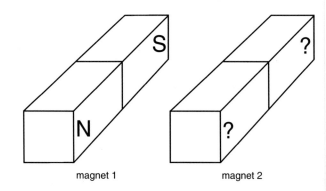

magnet 1   magnet 2

Explain how you would use magnet 1 to discover which end of magnet 2 is a north pole.

_____

_____

_____

3 marks

a)   In circuit 1 which bulb(s) will glow when switch S1 is closed?

_____

2 marks

b)   In circuit 2 which bulb(s) will glow when switch S2 is closed?

_____

2 marks

How much do you know? continued

3 The sentences below are about magnetic and non-magnetic materials.

Tick the box if you think the statement is true.

☐ A magnet will attract an iron rod.

☐ A magnet will not attract a steel nail.

☐ A magnet will attract a copper pipe.

☐ A magnet will not attract a piece of wood.

2 marks

4 The diagram below shows an electric bell

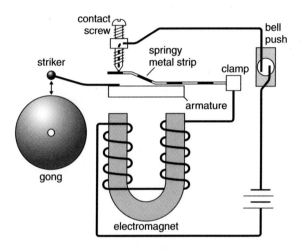

Explain why the hammer hits the bell when the button is pressed.

_____

_____

_____

2 marks

5 Jill connected up the circuit shown below. X and Y are identical bulbs.

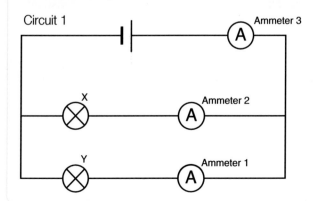

The current flowing through ammeter 1 is 0.1 A. What is the size of the current flowing through

a) Ammeter 2 _____A

b) Ammeter 3 _____A.

2 marks

c) Jill then altered the circuit by adding a second cell.

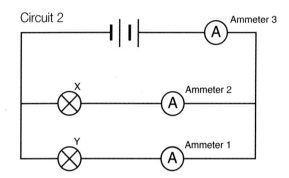

Tick the box to show which statement is correct.

☐ The current flowing through Ammeter 1 will be larger than that in circuit 1.

☐ The current flowing through Ammeter 1 will be smaller than that in circuit 1.

☐ The current flowing through Ammeter 1 will be the same as that in circuit 1.

1 mark

6 The diagram below shows two Christmas trees decorated with lights.

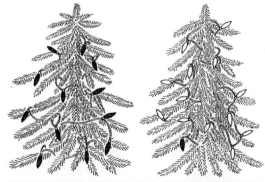

Both trees have one bulb which is broken. None of the lights on tree A are glowing. All of the lights on tree B, apart from the broken one, are glowing.

a) What kind of lighting circuit does tree A have?

_____

1 mark

b) What kind of lighting circuit does tree B have?

_____

1 mark

10.1 SPEED

Figure 1

The athlete in this photograph can travel 100 m in 10 s. On average he will travel 10 m each second. In other words his **average speed** is 10 m/s.

You can calculate the average speed of an object using the equation

$$\text{Speed} = \frac{\text{Distance travelled}}{\text{Time taken}}$$

In this example, speed $= \dfrac{100 \text{ m}}{10 \text{ s}}$

Average speed of sprinter = 10 m/s

Figure 2

Concorde travels 3000 km in just $1\frac{1}{2}$ hours.

$$\text{Speed} = \frac{\text{Distance travelled}}{\text{Time taken}}$$

$$\text{Speed} = \frac{3000 \text{ km}}{1.5 \text{ h}}$$

Average speed of Concorde = 2000 km/h

Figure 3

This cyclist took 5 s to travel 100 m.

$$\text{Speed} = \frac{\text{Distance travelled}}{\text{Time taken}}$$

$$\text{Speed} = \frac{100 \text{ m}}{5 \text{ s}}$$

His average speed = 20 m/s

The table below gives some typical speeds.

Light	300 000 000 m/s
Earth orbiting the Sun	2 200 000 m/s
Rifle bullet	approx. 700 m/s
Sound	340 m/s
Jumbo jet 747 (maximum speed)	270 m/s
Cheetah (maximum speed)	28 m/s
Olympic sprinter	12 m/s
Man walking briskly	1.3 m/s
Snail	approx. 0.001 m/s

Using graphs to show motion

It is often useful to show the movement of an object as a graph.

Distance–Time graphs

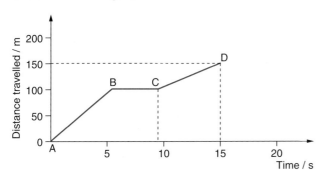

Figure 4 Distance–time graph **for a cyclist**

Figure 4 shows that the cyclist

- travels 100 m in 5 s between A and B
- is stationary for 4 s between B and C
- travels 50 m in 6 s between C and D.

Speed–Time graphs

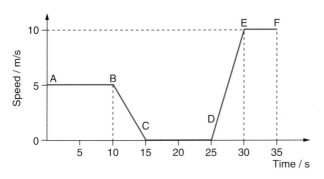

Figure 5 Speed–time graph **for a runner**

Figure 5 shows that the runner

- travels at a constant speed of 5 m/s for 10 s between A and B
- slows down between B and C
- is stationary for 10 s between C and D
- increases speed between D and E
- travels at a constant speed of 10 m/s for 5 s between E and F.

An object which increases its speed is **accelerating**.

Figure 6

Key terms

Check that you understand and can explain the following terms:

- ★ speed
- ★ average speed
- ★ distance–time graph
- ★ speed–time graph
- ★ accelerating
- ★ decelerating

Questions

1 Fill in the gaps in the table below.

	Distance travelled	Time taken	Average speed
1	10 cm	5 s	
2	20 m	4 s	
3	500 km	5 h	
4	750 km	3 h	
5	5 km	300 mins	
6	9 km	1.5 h	

2 Calculate the speed of the cyclist in Figure 4 between points

 a) A and B

 b) C and D.

3 Between which points in Figure 5 is the runner a) accelerating and b) decelerating?

An object which is slowing down is **decelerating**.

Figure 7

FORCES AND MOTION

115

10.2 FORCES

FORCES AND MOTION

Effects of forces

There are many different types of **force**. These include pushes, pulls, twists and stretches.

If you apply a force to an object it may

- make it start to move
- make it move faster
- slow it down
- make it stop
- change the direction in which it is moving
- change its shape.

These effects are illustrated below:

Figure 1

Sometimes it is not necessary to be **in contact** with an object in order to apply a force to it.

Figure 2 **Effect of gravity**

The bungee jumper in Figure 2 has just jumped out of the basket and is feeling the force of gravity pulling him downwards. The common name given to this force is **weight**.

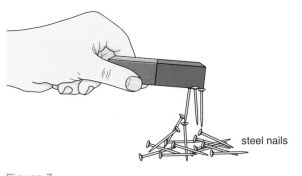

steel nails

Figure 3

The steel nails in Figure 3 are lifted by a force. This **attractive force** exists between magnets and magnetic materials such as iron and steel (see p 108).

Measuring forces

The size of a force is measured in **newtons**, usually shortened to **N** (named after Sir Isaac Newton).

If you hold a medium sized apple in your hand it will be pushing down with a force of approximately 1 N.

The sizes of some other forces are illustrated below:

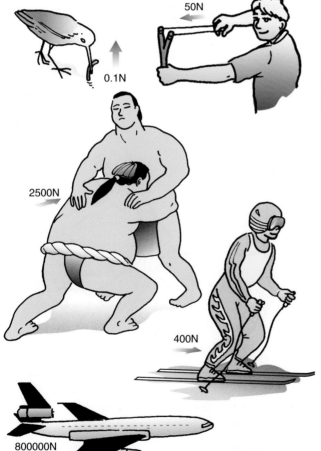

Figure 4

Key terms

Check that you understand and can explain the following terms:

★ force ★ attractive force
★ in contact ★ newton
★ weight ★ newtonmeter

Questions

1 Name five things that may happen to an object if a force is applied to it. Give one example for each.

2 Describe two situations in which a force is applied to an object without being in contact with it.

3 Find out how much force you apply to the floor when you are standing up. (Hint: 1 kg provides a force of approx. 10 N).

4 Draw a diagram of a newtonmeter and explain how it can be used to find the force necessary to open your classroom door.

Newtonmeter

We can measure the size of a force using a **newtonmeter**. The larger the force, the more the spring stretches.

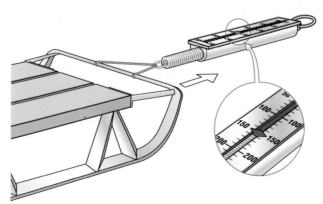

Figure 5 **A newtonmeter**

10.3 BALANCED AND UNBALANCED FORCES

In everyday life it is rare for an object to be acted upon by no forces or a single force. It is much more likely that it will experience several forces. These forces may be **balanced** or **unbalanced**.

Balanced forces

Figure 1

If the two tug of war teams in Figure 1 pull with the same force, the forces are balanced and there is no movement.

Unbalanced forces

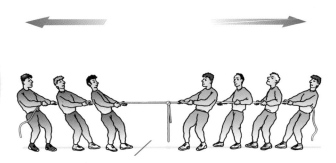

Figure 2

If one of the teams pulls with a force which is greater than that of the opposition, the forces are unbalanced and there is movement (Figure 2).

We can summarise this by saying that unbalanced forces produce change in the motion of an object, while balanced forces do not.

Effects of friction

One of the most common forces which can act upon an object is **friction**. Whenever an object moves or tries to move, friction is present.

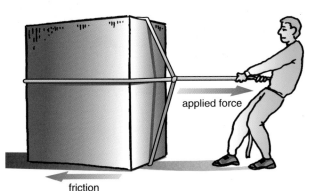

Friction always acts in the direction which opposes the motion.

Figure 3 **Friction always acts in the direction which opposes movement**

On some occasions friction can prove very useful. For example, when you walk or run, you push yourself forward by pushing backwards on the ground. Friction between your foot and the floor helps you to do this. If there was no friction, your feet would slip!

Figure 4 **The importance of friction**

Smooth surfaces reduce the friction between objects, while rough surfaces increase the **frictional forces**. In Figure 5, the trainers and football boots are designed to prevent your foot from slipping by increasing the frictional forces between you and the ground. In contrast, the skates and skis are designed with smooth surfaces which keep friction to a minimum.

Figure 5

Questions

1 Give one example of an object which is being acted upon by a) balanced forces and b) unbalanced forces. Draw diagrams to show the direction of the forces.

2 What is friction? Give two examples of situations in which friction is an advantage and two examples where it is a disadvantage.

3 How can the friction between two objects be a) increased and b) decreased?

4 Explain how air resistance slows down a parachutist as they fall.

In order that a car can change its speed or direction, there must be friction between its tyres and the road surface. A new tyre with lots of tread has a rough surface and will provide lots of grip. A worn tyre with a smoother surface will provide less grip and the car will be much more difficult to control.

Figure 6

Air resistance

The parachutist in Figure 7 relies upon the friction due to the air, known as **air resistance**, to prevent him from falling too fast.

1 When the parachute is first opened, the air resistance is large and the parachutist's descent is slowed down.

2 As his speed decreases, the air resistance lessens.

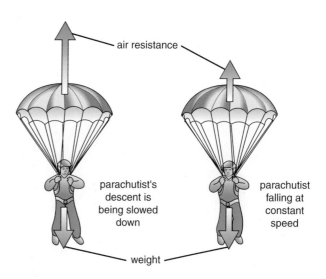

Figure 7

3 When the downward force and the air resistance are balanced, his speed remains constant. A parachute is designed so that the speed at which this balance occurs is slow enough to allow a parachutist to land safely.

10.4 FORCES AND PRESSURE

If you were to stand on someone's foot while wearing stiletto heels, you would cause them considerable pain as all your weight would be **concentrated** in a **small area**. If, however, you were to stand on someone's foot while wearing hiking boots, you would cause them considerably less pain as your weight would be spread over a large area.

Figure 1

If a force is concentrated into a small area it creates a **large pressure**. If a force is spread over a large area it creates a **small pressure**.

If you wear snowshoes whilst walking in snow your weight will be spread over a large area and you won't sink. Without the snowshoes the force is more concentrated and you are likely to sink.

Figure 2

You should NEVER walk across a frozen pond or lake. The pressure your weight creates may be sufficient to crack the ice. Rescuers can avoid this problem by using a long ladder which spreads their weight and so reduces the pressure they exert on the ice.

Figure 3

The pressure created at the point of this nail is large enough for the point to pierce the wood.

Figure 4

If the point is blunt, the pressure is less and the point will not pierce the wood.

Figure 5

Because there are a large number of nails on this fakir's bed, the pressure on each nail point is too small to pierce his skin.

Figure 6

Key terms

Check that you understand and can explain the following terms:

* ★ concentrated
* ★ small area
* ★ large pressure
* ★ small pressure
* ★ pascal (Pa)

Questions

1 Which of these shoes would create the greatest pressure: a) trainers, b) football boots, or c) skating boots?

2 Why do sprinters wear shoes that have spikes in their soles?

3 Why would a shopping bag with thin string for handles be painful to carry?

4 Why does a drawing pin have a large head?

5 A girl weighing 500 N is wearing shoes whose soles have a total surface area of 0.1 m^2. Calculate the pressure she creates beneath her feet.

Calculating pressure

The pressure created by a force can be calculated using the equation

$$\text{Pressure} = \frac{\text{Force}}{\text{Area}}$$

Pressure is measured in **pascals** (**Pa**). 1 Pa is the same as 1 N/m^2.

Examples

Figure 7 shows three crates of equal weight with different areas in contact with the ground. The dimensions are labelled in each case. An accompanying calculation shows how the pressure created by each crate is calculated.

(a)
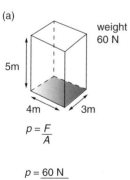
weight 60 N
5m
4m   3m

$p = \dfrac{F}{A}$

$p = \dfrac{60\ \text{N}}{12\ \text{m}^2}$

$p = 5\ \text{Pa}$

(b)
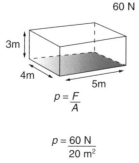
weight 60 N
3m
4m   5m

$p = \dfrac{F}{A}$

$p = \dfrac{60\ \text{N}}{20\ \text{m}^2}$

$p = 3\ \text{Pa}$

(c)
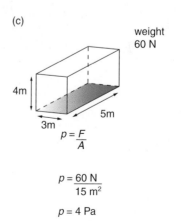
weight 60 N
4m
3m   5m

$p = \dfrac{F}{A}$

$p = \dfrac{60\ \text{N}}{15\ \text{m}^2}$

$p = 4\ \text{Pa}$

Figure 7

10.5 TURNING FORCES

FORCES AND MOTION

Sometimes when you apply a force to an object you can make it turn or rotate. The **turning effect** of a force is called a **moment**. Figure 1 illustrates some examples of the turning effect of forces.

The size of the turning effect depends upon

◆ the size of the force you apply
◆ the place where it is applied.

The point around which the force is turning is called the **pivot**.

If you apply a force a long way from the pivot you can create a large moment.

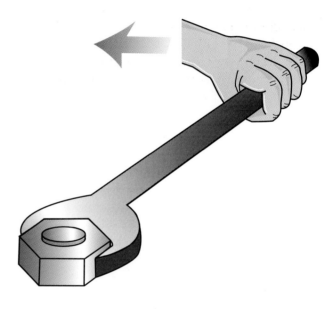

Figure 2 **Creating a large moment**

If you apply a similar force close to the pivot the moment created will be smaller.

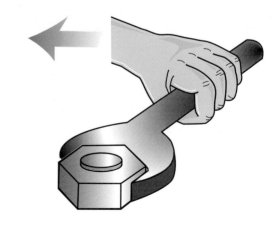

Figure 3 **Creating a smaller moment**

This explains why it is easier to undo a stiff nut using a long spanner.

122

Figure 1

The turning effect of a force can be calculated using the equation

> Moment of a force = Force × Distance from pivot

The moment created by the long spanner was 100 N × 0.5 m = 50 Nm.

The moment created by the short spanner was 100 N × 0.2 m = 20 Nm.

Balancing moments

When this girl sits on the see-saw (Figure 4) her weight creates a moment which tries to turn the see-saw clockwise. Her friend's weight on the opposite side of the see-saw creates an even larger moment which turns the see-saw anticlockwise. The moments and the see-saw are unbalanced.

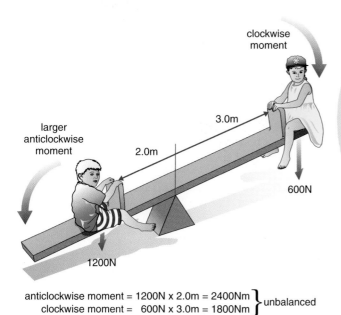

anticlockwise moment = 1200N x 2.0m = 2400Nm ⎫
clockwise moment = 600N x 3.0m = 1800Nm ⎭ unbalanced

Figure 4

If the boy moves forward so he is 1.5 m from the centre, the see-saw will balance because

> **anticlockwise moment = clockwise moment**.

anticlockwise = 1200N x 1.5m = 1800Nm ⎫
moment ⎬ balanced
clockwise = 600N x 3.0m = 1800Nm ⎭
moment

This is called the **principle of moments**.

Key terms

Check that you understand and can explain the following terms:

★ moment
★ pivot
★ turning effect
★ moment of a force
★ balancing moments
★ clockwise moment
★ anticlockwise moment
★ principle of moments

Questions

1 Give three examples of forces which create a turning effect.

2 Why is it easier to open a tin of paint using a long screwdriver than a short screwdriver?

3 What is a pivot? Draw a diagram to illustrate your answer.

4 A man opens a door by pushing with a force of 50 N at a point 0.5 m from the hinges. Calculate the moment he creates.

5 Give one example of two moments which are balanced.

In Indian wrestling you try to push your opponent's hand down on to the table without lifting or moving his elbow. The force exerted by the winner causes both arms to turn about the elbows. If the contest is evenly balanced, there will be no movement as the clockwise moments will equal the anticlockwise moments.

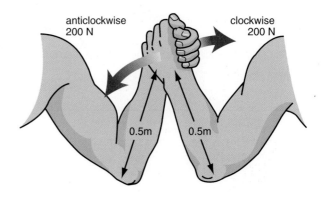

Figure 5 **Balanced moments**

What you need to know!

1 The speed of an object can be found using the equation, Speed = Distance travelled/Time taken.

2 Pulls, pushes and twists are all different kinds of forces.

3 The size of a force is measured in newtons (N).

4 Weight is the force exerted on an object due to the pull of gravity.

5 If several forces act upon an object, they may be balanced or unbalanced.

6 Unbalanced forces cause an object to change its motion.

7 Friction is a force which opposes motion.

8 Some forces cause objects to turn or rotate.

9 The turning effect of a force is called a moment.

10 Pressure describes how a force is spread and can be calculated using the equation,
Pressure = Force/Area.

How much do you know?

1 A rocketman is travelling forwards at a constant speed.

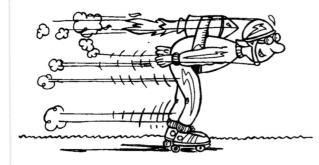

a) Tick the box which describes what happens to his speed when the rocket motor is turned on (as shown in the diagram above).

He continues at the same speed ☐
He slows down ☐
He goes faster ☐

1 mark

b) The rocketman travels 40 m in just 8 s.

Calculate his average speed.

_____

_____

2 marks

2 The graph opposite shows the journey of a cyclist.

a) How long did the whole journey take?

_____

1 mark

b) What was the greatest speed the cyclist reached?

_____

1 mark

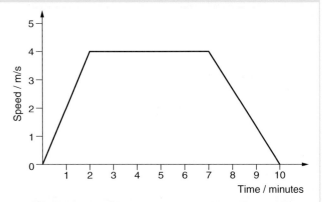

c) For how long was the cyclist travelling at a constant speed?

_____

1 mark

3 The diagram below shows a wagon moving at a constant speed and the forces which are being applied to it.

frictional forces

force from engine

a) What happens to the wagon if the frictional forces become greater than the pull of the engine?

_____

1 mark

How much do you know? continued

b) What happens if the frictional forces are less than the pull of the engine?

_____

1 mark

4 The photo below shows a golf ball being hit by a golf club.

What can you see in the photo which shows that the club must be applying a force to the ball?

_____

1 mark

5 The diagram below shows a spanner being used to undo a nut on a car wheel.

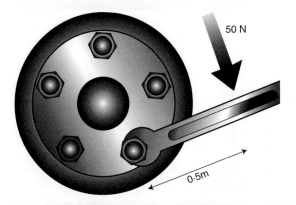

50 N

0·5m

a) Calculate the size of the moment created by the 50 N force.

_____

_____

_____

3 marks

b) If the nut was stiff and you needed to create a larger moment using the same force, what would you do?

_____

1 mark

6 The diagram below shows two friends Janet and John on a see-saw. Janet and John both weigh the same.

What should John do in order to balance the see-saw?

_____

_____

2 marks

7 Two girls of equal weight walk across a snow-covered field. One is wearing snowshoes, the other is not.

a) Explain why the girl wearing snowshoes is able to walk on top of the snow but the girl without the snowshoes sinks deep into the snow.

_____

_____

3 marks

b) The girl wearing the snowshoes weighs 500 N. The total area of her two snowshoes is 0.5 m^2.

Calculate the pressure exerted by the snowshoes on the snow.

_____

_____

2 marks

RAYS OF LIGHT AND REFLECTION

The importance of light

Figure 1

You see objects because rays of light from **luminous** sources, such as the Sun, light bulbs and fires, are **reflected** into your eyes. If there is no light entering your eye, you are unable to see.

How does light travel?

On a bright day when the Sun shines through the clouds, you might notice that rays of light travel in straight lines.

Figure 2 **Light travels in straight lines**

Light travels very very quickly – at 300 000 000 metres per second. It takes a ray of light just 8 minutes to travel from the Sun to the Earth.

How are shadows formed?

Transparent objects, such as a sheet of glass, allow light to travel through them. **Opaque** objects, such as a sheet of card, do not allow light to pass through.

Figure 3 **Light can only travel through transparent objects**

If an opaque object is placed in front of a source of light, an area of darkness called a **shadow** is created. The shape of the shadow is the same as the shape of the object. This supports the idea that light travels in straight lines.

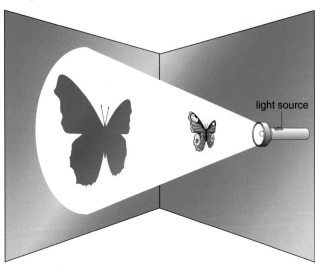

light source

Figure 4 **How a shadow is created**

Reflection of light

When a ray of light strikes a flat or plane surface it is always reflected at the same angle. In other words, the **angle of incidence** is equal to the **angle of reflection**.

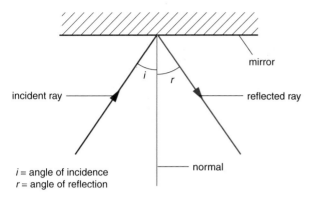

i = angle of incidence
r = angle of reflection

Figure 5 **The reflection of light**

A simple **periscope** makes use of this idea so that you can see over high objects or round corners.

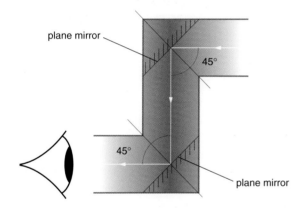

Figure 6 **A simple periscope**

Why do some flat objects look glossy when light shines on them and others look dull?

Shiny surfaces

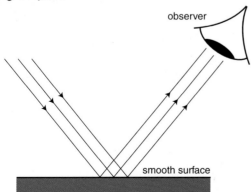

Figure 7

Key terms

Check that you understand and can explain the following terms:

★ luminous
★ reflect
★ transparent
★ opaque
★ shadow
★ angle of incidence
★ angle of reflection
★ periscope
★ shiny surface
★ dull surface

Questions

1 Give two examples of a luminous source of light.

2 Why are you unable to see when you close your eyes?

3 Give two examples of transparent objects.

4 Give two examples of opaque objects.

5 Draw a diagram of a periscope and explain how you might use it to see over a wall.

6 Explain with diagrams why shoes which have been polished look shiny but shoes which have not been polished look dull.

The smooth surface of a mirror or a table appears **shiny** because a lot of the reflected rays enter your eyes.

Dull surfaces

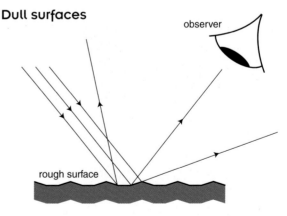

Figure 8

Rough surfaces scatter the rays, so fewer of them enter your eyes and the surface appears **dull**.

127

11.2 REFRACTION AND COLOUR

Light is able to travel through many different materials such as air, water, glass and perspex. These materials are called **media**. When a ray travels between media, it often changes direction as it crosses the boundary. This changing of direction is called **refraction**. It happens because the light changes speed as it crosses the boundary.

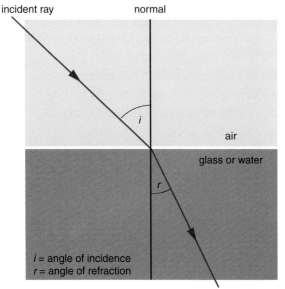

incident ray normal

i

air

glass or water

r

i = angle of incidence
r = angle of refraction

refracted ray bends towards normal

Figure 1

A ray of light travelling from air into glass or water slows down and bends *towards* the **normal**.

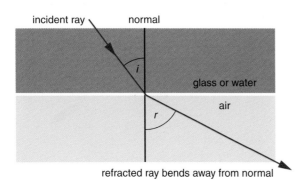

incident ray normal

i

glass or water

air

r

refracted ray bends away from normal

Figure 2

A ray travelling from glass or water into air speeds up and bends *away* from the normal.

Effects of refraction

Because our brains and our eyes believe that light travels in straight lines, refraction can cause some strange optical illusions.

If you place a pencil in a beaker of water it appears to be bent. This happens because the rays of light from the part of the pencil under the water change direction as they cross the water/air boundary.

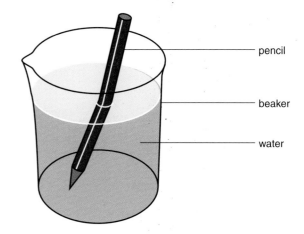

pencil

beaker

water

Figure 3 **The pencil appears to be bent because of the refraction of light**

Dispersion of white light

If you shine a ray of white light into a glass prism you will see it refract as it enters and as it leaves. These refractions cause the white light to split into a band of colours called a **spectrum**. This effect is called **dispersion**.

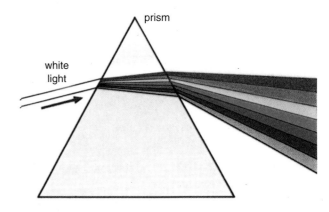

prism

white
light

Figure 4 **The spectrum**

This experiment shows that white light is a mixture of coloured lights – the colours of the rainbow. The colours in order are red, orange, yellow, green, blue, indigo and violet. The order is easily remembered by the saying, **R**ichard **O**f **Y**ork **G**ave **B**attle **I**n **V**ain.

Coloured objects

Most objects have some colour, for example grass is green, ink is blue. They have these colours because they contain a chemical called a **dye**. The dye **absorbs** all the colours of light which strike it except for its own colour which is reflected.

Figure 5

For example, when white light from the Sun hits the red car in Figure 5, all the colours are absorbed except for red. This is reflected into your eyes so the car looks red.

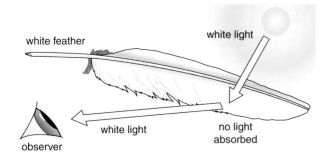

Figure 6

Figure 6 shows that when white light from the Sun hits the white feather, none of the colours are absorbed. As they are all reflected into your eyes, the feather looks white.

Coloured filters

A **filter** is a clear piece of plastic which has been coloured by a dye. Light which is the same colour as the filter can pass through it but other colours cannot.

Key terms

Check that you understand and can explain the following terms:

* media
* refraction
* normal
* dispersion
* spectrum
* dye
* absorb
* filter

Questions

1 Draw a diagram to show what happens to a ray of light when it a) travels from glass into air and b) travels from air into glass.

2 Name an everyday effect of refraction.

3 Name the colours of the rainbow in order.

4 Explain with a diagram why a blue book appears to be blue when white light shines on it.

5 Explain with a diagram what happens when white light tries to pass through a blue filter.

In Figure 7, red light can pass through the red filter but the orange, yellow, green, blue, indigo and violet cannot.

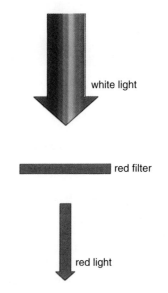

Figure 7

11.3 CREATING SOUNDS

Every sound you hear is made by an object which is **vibrating**. These sounds travel outwards from the source as **waves**.

Figure 1 illustrates this idea.

Figure 1

◆ The skin on the drum vibrates to produce the sound of the drum beat.
◆ When the clanger hits the inside of the bell, the vibrations are heard as a ringing sound.
◆ The buzzing sound you hear from a bee is created by the vibration of its wings.
◆ In the loudspeaker, electrical energy is changed into vibrations which we hear as sounds or music.

Frequency of vibration and pitch

If an object is large, like one of the strings of this double bass, it will vibrate slowly when you pluck it and you will hear a deep, **low pitched** sound.

double bass

Figure 2 **Low pitched sounds seen on an oscilloscope**

It is possible for you to *see* these waves using a piece of apparatus called a cathode ray oscilloscope (CRO).

Because the strings are vibrating slowly, just a few waves are produced each second. The waves have a **low frequency**.

If an object is small, like a violin string, it will vibrate quickly when you pluck it and produce **high pitched** sounds.

violin

Figure 3 **Higher pitched sounds seen on an oscilloscope**

Because the strings vibrate quickly, they produce lots of waves each second. The waves have a **high frequency**.

> Small objects vibrate quickly producing high pitched sounds.
> Large objects vibrate slowly producing low pitched sounds.

Hearing range

Some objects vibrate so quickly you may be unable to hear the sounds they produce. For example, bats hunt and communicate with each other by high pitched squeals which humans cannot hear. These are called **ultra sounds**.

Figure 4 **A bat detects its prey using ultra sound**

Some objects vibrate so slowly they also produce sounds you may not be able to hear. For example, many of the sounds which elephants make cannot be heard by humans as their pitch is too low.

Questions

1 All sounds begin with an object which is _____.

2 Write down the names of four musical instruments you would find in an orchestra. Which of these instruments would produce high pitched notes and which would produce low pitched notes? Explain your answers.

3 Draw a diagram to show the kind of picture you would see on a CRO if the note being played is
a) low pitched
b) high pitched.

4 Name two animals that can hear sounds which are outside the human hearing range.

Figure 5 **Elephants often communicate using very low-pitched sounds**

The range of frequencies that can be heard varies a little from person to person. Older people usually have a narrower **hearing range** than the young.

131

11.4 SOUND WAVES

LIGHT AND SOUND

Loudness and amplitude of vibration

If an object vibrates with a large **amplitude** it will produce a loud sound. This is seen on the CRO as a **tall wave** (Figure 1).

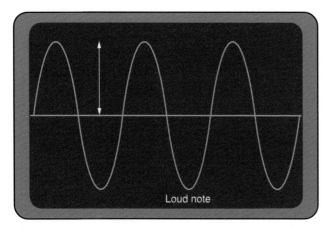

Loud note

Figure 1

A wave like this could be produced by hitting a drum skin hard.

If you hit the skin of a drum gently it will vibrate with a small amplitude producing a **soft or quiet** sound. This is seen on the CRO as a wave which is small in height (Figure 2).

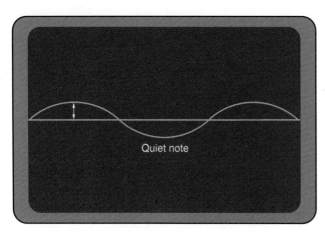

Quiet note

Figure 2

Loudness and the decibel scale

Very loud noises, such as those made by aircraft, machinery in factories, heavy goods lorries and personal stereos with the volume turned up high, can damage your hearing. The **loudness** of a sound is measured on the **decibel scale**.

Type of sound	Average loudness (dB)
A bird singing quietly	20
People talking reasonably quietly	60
A dog howling close by	80
A noisy factory	90
Someone playing the trumpet	100
A noisy disco	110
A jet aircraft taking off	130
A bomb exploding	more than 150

Sound waves

Sounds travel from vibrating objects to your ears by means of **sound waves**.

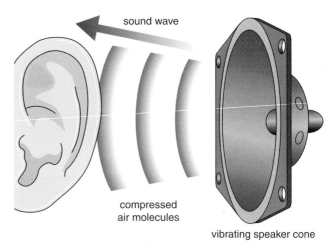

sound wave

compressed air molecules

vibrating speaker cone

Figure 3 **Sound waves**

As an object vibrates back and forth it pushes the surrounding air molecules, creating sound waves which travel outwards in all directions. When these waves enter the ear they make the **ear drum** vibrate. These vibrations are **amplified** (made larger) by three connected bones (hammer, anvil and stirrup) and then passed along the **auditory nerves** to the brain.

Simple Telephone

If you speak into one of the cups, your partner will be able to clearly hear what you are saying. Your sound waves will travel along the string between the cups.

Figure 4 **A simple telephone**

Questions

1 Draw a diagram of the picture you would expect to see on a CRO for a) a loud note and b) a quiet note.

2 What number on the decibel scale would you record for a) a jet aircraft taking off close by and b) two people having a normal conversation?

3 What might happen to your hearing if you are exposed to very loud sounds for a long period of time? Give two examples of places where you might find these very loud sounds.

4 Explain why it is not possible for sounds to travel through a vacuum.

Sounds are able to travel through solids and gases. They can also travel though liquids such as water, which explains how whales and dolphins are able to communicate with each other. For sound to be able to travel, there must be molecules present. Sound *cannot travel through a **vacuum***.

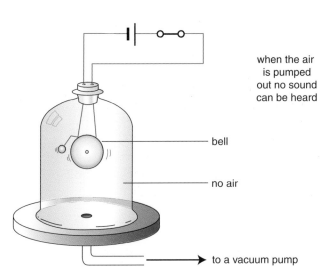

when the air is pumped out no sound can be heard

bell

no air

to a vacuum pump

Figure 5 **The bell jar experiment showing that sound cannot travel through a vacuum**

The bell jar experiment
When there is air in this bell jar you will be able to see and hear the bell ringing. If you then pump the air out of the jar and turn on the bell you will see it working but you will not be able to hear it. There are no molecules in the jar to carry the sound energy.

Speed of sound
Sound waves travel much more slowly than light waves (see page 126). This is why you always see a flash of lightning before you hear thunder.

What you need to know!

1   The Sun, stars and fires are all sources of light. They are luminous objects.

2   We see non-luminous objects because light is reflected from them into our eyes.

3   Light travels in straight lines.

4   Light travels much faster than sound.

5   Shadows are areas of darkness created when opaque objects are placed in front of a source of light.

6   Flat surfaces, such as plane mirrors, reflect light in a predictable direction.

7   Refraction may cause white light to split into the colours of the rainbow.

8   Rays of light may refract as they cross the boundary between two different media.

9   Coloured objects absorb all the colours of the spectrum except their own, which is reflected.

10 Coloured filters absorb all the colours of the spectrum except their own, which they allow to pass through.

11 Sounds are made when objects vibrate.

12 The greater the amplitude of vibration, the louder the sound.

13 The higher the frequency of vibration, the higher the pitch of the sound.

14 Sound energy travels in waves.

15 Sounds can travel through solids, liquids and gases but not through a vacuum.

16 Sound waves cause the ear drum to vibrate.

17 Loud sounds can damage the ear drum and cause deafness.

18 Different people have different hearing ranges.

How much do you know?

1   Why is it that the boy wearing the blindfold in the diagram below is unable to see any of the other people in the room?

_____

_____

2 marks

2   The diagram diagonally opposite shows a ray of light striking a plane (flat) mirror. Which letter, A, B, C or D, shows the direction in which the ray will be reflected by the mirror.

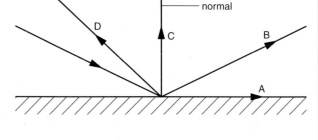

1 mark

3   Complete the diagram below showing how the rays of light striking this bicycle reflector are reflected.

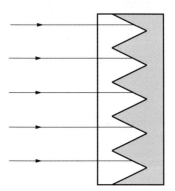

2 marks

How much do you know? continued

4 The diagram below shows a ray of white light striking a glass prism.

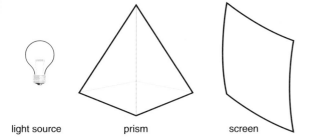

light source   prism   screen

a) What is seen on the white screen?

_____

1 mark

b) A red filter is placed between the prism and the screen. What is now seen on the white screen?

_____

1 mark

5 The diagram below shows a young girl watching a firework display.

Why does she see the flash of an exploding rocket before she hears the bang?

_____

_____

2 marks

6 The gong in the diagram below is vibrating gently and producing a quiet sound.

hammer   vibrating gong

a) What would you do to the gong to make it produce a loud sound?

_____

1 mark

b) Which of these two bells would you shake if you wanted to produce a lower-pitched sound?

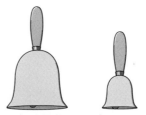

_____

1 mark

7 Richard likes to listen to loud music.

a) What may happen to Richard's hearing if he does this too often?

_____

1 mark

b) What two things could Richard do to avoid this problem?

_____

_____

2 marks

12.1 THE EARTH IN SPACE

You, your family, all your friends, in fact all mankind live on a **planet** called Earth. If you could see the Earth from space it would look like this.

Figure 1 **How the Earth looks from space**

This photograph shows Europe, the Atlantic Ocean and the Mediterranean Sea. Part of the Earth's surface is covered by cloud.

The daily journey of the Sun

Although you cannot feel it, the Earth is spinning around on its **axis** like a top. This turning motion makes the Sun appear to rise in the East, travel high overhead and then set in the West. The Earth completes one full turn or rotation every 24 hours – this is **one day**.

Day and night

As the Earth turns, part of its surface is in daylight whilst other parts are in darkness. It is **daytime** on those parts of the Earth that are receiving light from the Sun and **night** on those parts that are not receiving light from the Sun.

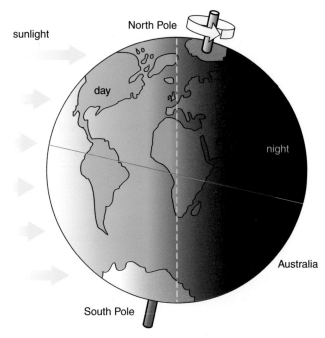

Figure 3 **The explanation for day and night**

Figure 2 **The Sun makes the same journey across the sky every day, but it is much lower in the sky in the winter**

Summer

East   West

Winter

East   West

A year and the seasons

The nearest **star** to the Earth is the **Sun**. It is 150 million kilometres away. The Earth **orbits** the Sun once every **year**, following a path called an **ellipse**. (An ellipse is a slightly squashed circle.)

As the Earth travels around the Sun we experience the different **seasons**. Seasonal changes to the weather and to the climate happen because the Earth's axis is slightly tilted.

When we in Britain are in **summer**, our part of the Earth (the northern part) is tilted towards the Sun. This makes our weather warmer and our days (time in daylight) longer.

When we are in **winter**, our part of the Earth is tilted away from the Sun. This makes our weather colder and our daytime shorter.

When we are in spring or autumn, our part of the Earth is tilted neither towards nor away from the Sun.

Key terms

Check that you understand and can explain the following terms:

★ planet	★ star/Sun
★ axis	★ orbit
★ one day	★ ellipse
★ daytime	★ season
★ night	★ summer
★ year	★ winter

Questions

1 What causes the Sun to appear each day in the east, travel across the sky and set in the west?

2 A day is the time it takes the Earth to _____.

3 A year is the time it takes the Earth to _____.

4 Explain, with diagrams, why parts of the Earth are in daylight whilst other parts are in darkness.

5 Explain, with diagrams, how the seasons change in the northern parts of the Earth.

Figure 4 **The explanation for the seasons**

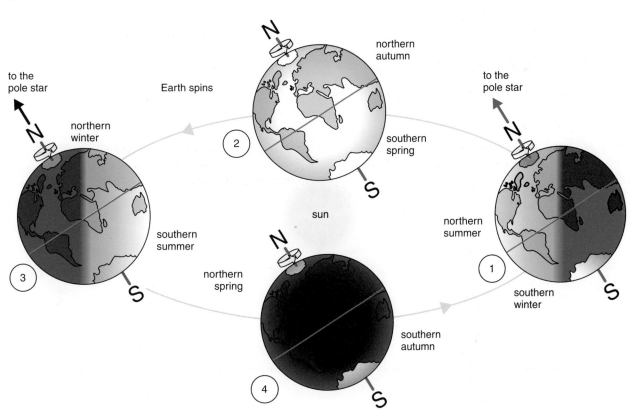

THE SOLAR SYSTEM

Planets

The Sun, the planets and their moons make up the **solar system**.

The Earth is just one of nine **planets** in the solar system which orbit the Sun. Starting with the planet nearest the Sun they are Mercury, Venus, Earth, Mars, Jupiter, Saturn, Uranus, Neptune and Pluto. Try using this sentence to help you remember the order. **M**any **V**ery **E**nergetic **M**en **J**og **S**lowly **U**pto **N**ewport **P**agnell.

It is not possible to draw this diagram to scale and fit it on this page but the diagram should give you some idea of the sizes of the planets and their distances from the Sun.

The table opposite gives some information about the planets in the solar system.

All the planets in the solar system move in **elliptical orbits**. They do this because of the strong pulling forces between the planets and the Sun. These forces are **forces of gravity** and they control the positions and the movements of the planets. The planets closest to the Sun feel the largest force and travel much quicker than those further away from the Sun.

Moons

Moons are natural objects which orbit a planet. The Earth has just one moon but Jupiter has 16 moons, Saturn has 23 moons and Mars and Venus have no moons.

Our moon orbits the Earth once every 28 days (a **lunar month**). It, like the planets, is kept in orbit by the pull of gravity.

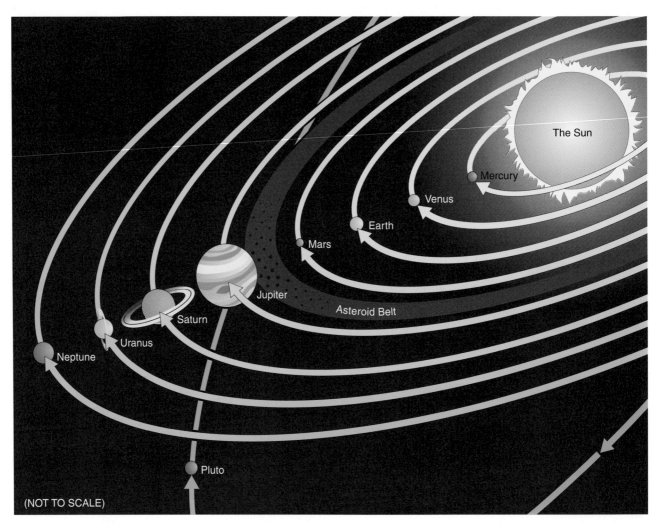

(NOT TO SCALE)

Figure 1 **The solar system**

Figure 2 **The Moon reflects the light from the Sun**

Key terms

Check that you understand and can explain the following terms:

- ★ solar system
- ★ planet
- ★ elliptical orbits
- ★ forces of gravity
- ★ moon
- ★ lunar month

Questions

1 What is the solar system?

2 Write down the names of all the planets in order starting from the planet closest to the Sun.

3 What is the shape of a planet's orbit around the Sun? What is the name of the force which makes the planets orbit the Sun?

4 Which is the largest planet in the solar system?

5 Which is the smallest planet in the solar system?

6 What is a moon? Which planet has 16 moons?

Planet	Approximate distance from the Sun compared with the Earth	Approximate diameter compared with the Earth	Time to orbit the Sun in years
Mercury	0.5	0.5	0.2
Venus	0.75	1	0.6
Earth	1	1	1
Mars	1.5	0.5	1.9
Jupiter	5	11	11.9
Saturn	10	10	29.5
Uranus	19	4	84
Neptune	30	3.5	165
Pluto	40	0.2	248

Stars

Stars are luminous objects, i.e. they give out light. The star at the centre of our solar system is the Sun. During the daytime, the light from the Sun is so bright that it is impossible to see any other stars. They only become visible as the Sun sets. These other stars seem very small and dim compared with the Sun, because they are much, much further away.

Planets and moons can also be seen in the night sky but they are not luminous objects. We see them because they reflect the light from the Sun.

Figure 1 **The sky at night**

Constellations

Groups of suns or stars which appear close together in the sky are called **constellations**. You will probably have heard of some of them and can perhaps identify their shape.

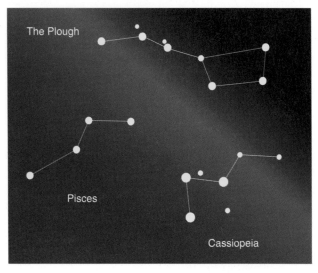

The Plough

Pisces

Cassiopeia

Figure 2 **Some well-known constellations**

Galaxies

Stars and constellations cluster together in enormous groups called **galaxies**. Our galaxy is called the Milky Way and contains about 200 million stars. There are billions of galaxies spread throughout the universe.

Figure 3 **The Milky Way**

The moving night sky

If you were to take a photograph of the stars in the sky every hour, you would discover that they appear to revolve and change position. This happens because the Earth is rotating. Only one star, the Pole Star, appears not to move, as it is directly above the axis of rotation.

Artificial satellites

The moon orbits the Earth – it is a **natural satellite**. There are many man-made objects which also orbit the Earth and these are called **artificial satellites**. These artificial satellites have many uses.

1 Observing the Earth from above. For example, weather satellites provide information which makes weather forecasting more reliable.

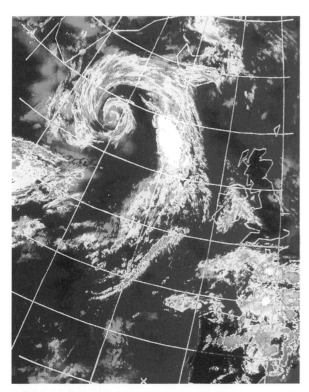

Figure 4 **This photograph from a weather satellite shows how weather fronts are moving**

Questions

1 What is a luminous object?

2 Why is it not possible to see stars during the day?

3 Planets and moons are non-luminous objects and yet we can see them in the night sky. Explain why we are able to do this.

4 What are constellations?

5 Sketch a diagram of a) the Plough and b) Pisces.

6 Why do these stars seem to change their position during the night?

7 Name one natural and one artificial satellite.

2 Allowing communication between people all over the world using radio, television or the internet.

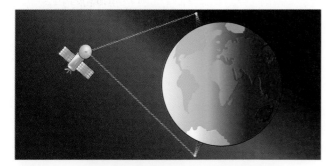

Figure 5 **When the radio signal arrives at the satellite, it is redirected down to another part of the Earth where the message is received**

3 Looking away from the Earth into space, to help us learn more about the solar system and the universe.

When scientists use telescopes to observe objects in space, they have to look through the Earth's atmosphere and this may prevent them from seeing objects clearly. They have recently overcome this problem by mounting a telescope on a satellite which is orbiting above the Earth's atmosphere. This telescope is called the Hubble telescope. It is orbiting 600 kilometres above the Earth's surface.

Figure 6 **The Hubble telescope**

What you need to know!

1 Because the Earth is spinning, the position of the Sun appears to change throughout the day.

2 As a result of this spinning motion, parts of our planet are in darkness whilst other parts are in sunlight. It is night where the Earth's surface is in darkness and day where the surface is receiving light from the Sun.

3 It takes one day for the Earth to rotate once.

4 It takes one year for the Earth to orbit the Sun once.

5 The seasons change as the Earth orbits the Sun.

6 The Sun is at the centre of our solar system.

7 There are nine orbiting planets in our solar system.

8 The Sun and the stars are sources of light. Non-luminous bodies like the planets and moons are seen because of reflected light.

9 As the Earth spins and orbits the Sun, the positions of the stars in the night sky change.

10 The moon is a natural satellite.

11 The movements and positions of all the planets in our solar system are controlled by the pull of gravity (gravitational forces).

12 Artificial satellites can be used to observe the Earth, for example weather satellites, or to look away from the Earth, for example the Hubble telescope.

How much do you know?

1 The drawing below shows the positions of the Sun at different times during the day in the summer.
The circle marked A shows the position of the Sun early in the morning.

a) Write the letter B in the circle which shows where the Sun will be at midday.

_____

1 mark

b) Write the letter C in the circle which shows the position of the Sun in the late evening.

_____

1 mark

c) Draw a circle in the above diagram and write the letter D in it to show the position of the Sun at midday in the winter.

_____

1 mark

2 The diagram below shows sunlight shining onto part of the Earth.

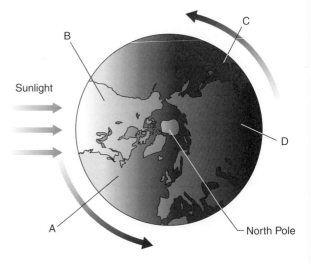

a) At which two places is it daytime?

_____

2 marks

b) At which two places is it night?

_____

2 marks

c) At which place is the Sun setting?

_____

1 mark

How much do you know? continued

3 The diagram below shows the positions of the Earth at different times of the year.

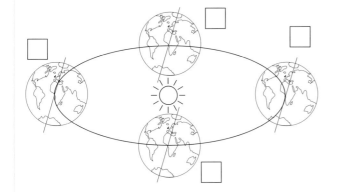

a) Put an A into the box which shows the position of the Earth when we are in summer.

1 mark

b) Put a B in the box which shows the position of the Earth when we are in winter.

1 mark

4 Look carefully at the information contained in the table below.

a) Which planet is furthest from the Sun?

_____

1 mark

b) Which planet is nearest the Sun?

_____

1 mark

Planet	Approximate distance from the Sun compared with the Earth	Approximate diameter compared with the Earth
Mercury	0.5	0.5
Venus	0.75	1
Earth	1	1
Mars	1.5	0.5
Jupiter	5	11
Saturn	10	10
Uranus	19	4
Neptune	30	3.5
Pluto	40	0.2

c) Which is the largest planet?

_____

1 mark

d) Which is the smallest planet?

_____

1 mark

e) Which planet should be the hottest?

_____

1 mark

f) Which planet will feel the largest gravitational forces?

_____

1 mark

5 Use words from this list to complete the sentences below.

planets	moons	satellites
Sun	gravity	galaxy
orbits	luminous	reflect

a) Our solar system has nine _____ which travel around the _____ in circular-like _____ .

3 marks

b) A large cluster of stars, such as the Milky Way is called a _____ .

1 mark

c) Stars give out light. They are _____ . Planets and _____ are non-luminous. We see them because of the light they_____ .

3 marks

6 Look at the list below

Earth	A
Moon	B
Sun	C
Constellation	D
Universe	E
Solar system	F

Put them in order of size from smallest to largest. The smallest one has already been done for you.

B _____

5 marks

The need for energy

You need **energy** every day of your life to run, to walk, to play and even to sleep. You receive all this energy from the food you eat.

Figure 1 **How you get energy**

Trees and plants need energy to grow and reproduce. They get most of their energy from the Sun.

Figure 2 **How a plant gets energy**

Machines need energy to be able to work. There are many ways in which machines can be given this energy.

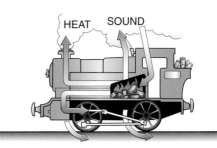

Figure 3 **The energy needed to move this train comes from burning coal**

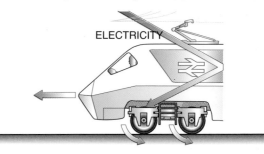

The energy needed to move this train comes from overhead electric cables

The energy needed to work this toy comes from the wound-up spring

Different kinds of energy

There are several different kinds of energy. These are listed below along with an example of each:

- **heat** or **thermal** energy – from a burning match

- **light** energy – from a torch

- **sound** energy – from a radio

- **electrical** energy – from batteries

◆ **chemical** energy – from fuels like petrol

◆ **nuclear** energy – from the centres of atoms

◆ **potential** or positional energy – objects can have potential energy because of their position. For example, a bag of flour over a door has gravitational potential energy because of its height above the ground.
An object can also have strain potential energy because of the shape it has been forced into, for example the bow of a bow and arrow

◆ **kinetic** or movement energy – objects which are moving have kinetic energy, for example a rocket

Energy transfers

When energy is used it does not disappear. It changes into a different form of energy.

Energy at the start	Energy changer	Energy after
Chemical (in the wax)	Candle	Heat and light
Electrical energy	Radio	Sound
Electrical energy	Electric fire	Light and heat
Strain energy	Catapult	Kinetic energy
Kinetic energy	Dynamo	Electrical energy
Electrical energy	Electric motor	Kinetic energy
Light energy	Green plants	Chemical energy
Chemical energy	Battery	Electrical energy

Key terms

Check that you understand and can explain the following terms:

★ energy
★ heat or thermal energy
★ light energy
★ sound energy
★ electrical energy
★ chemical energy
★ nuclear energy
★ potential energy
★ kinetic energy
★ energy transfer
★ concentrated

Questions

1 Name six different types of energy. Give one example of a source for each of these six types of energy.

2 Explain the energy transfer that takes place with a) a battery, b) a radio, c) a television, d) a bow and arrow, e) a wood fire and f) a clock-work car.

3 What device would change

   a) electrical energy into heat or thermal energy
   b) electrical energy into sound energy
   c) chemical energy into kinetic energy
   d) heat or thermal energy into kinetic energy
   e) light energy into chemical energy
   f) light energy into electrical energy?

4 Why are some forms of energy less useful after an energy transfer?

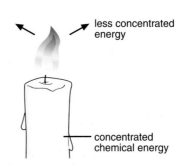

Figure 4

Although energy is never lost, it often changes into a less **concentrated** form which is not easy to use again. For example, the wax of a candle is a concentrated source of chemical energy but the light and heat which it changes into is much less concentrated and is therefore difficult to re-use.

13.2 ENERGY RESOURCES

The pie chart in Figure 1 shows how different **energy resources** were used in 1996.

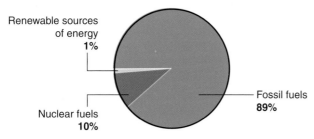

Renewable sources of energy **1%**

Nuclear fuels **10%**

Fossil fuels **89%**

Figure 1

During that year nearly 90% of the UK's energy needs came from the **fossil fuels** – coal, oil and gas. If we continue to use these valuable fuels at this rate, they will soon be gone.

Coal, oil and gas are **non-renewable** sources of energy. This means that once they have been used up, they cannot be replaced.

How are fossil fuels formed?

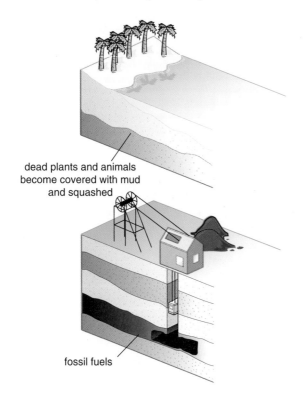

dead plants and animals become covered with mud and squashed

fossil fuels

Figure 2

Millions of years ago plants and animals died and fell to the bottom of lakes and seas where they became covered with mud (Figure 2a).

Over a very long period of time more and more layers of mud formed, creating enormous pressures which gradually changed the dead plants and animals into coal, oil or gas (Figure 2b).

A **fuel** releases its energy when it is burned. The most common fuels include coal, oil, gas and wood.

To avoid running out of fossil fuels we must use them more efficiently and we must look for **alternative sources of energy** which are **renewable**.

Renewable sources of energy

1   **Wind energy**   This has been used for many hundreds of years to pump water or to turn the millstones which produced flour. Nowadays, efficient generators change the energy of the wind into electrical energy. This is a very useful source of energy for isolated communities with no national electrical supply.

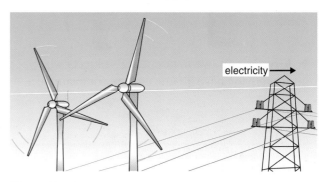

electricity →

Figure 3   **Wind energy**

2   **Hydroelectric energy**   Rain water stored behind a dam has potential energy. When it is released, the water's energy can be used to drive turbines and generators to produce electricity (see page 148).

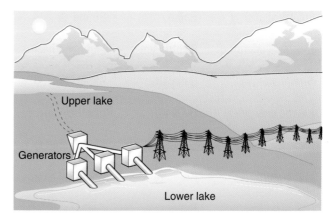

Upper lake

Generators

Lower lake

Figure 4   **Hydroelectric energy**

3 Tidal energy   The Moon and the Sun cause waters around the world to rise and fall. If the water is trapped behind a barrier when the tide is high and released when the tide is low, its potential energy can be used like hydroelectric energy.

4 Solar energy   Most of the Earth's energy comes from the Sun. This solar energy can be converted directly into electricity using photocells like that seen in the calculator in Figure 5.

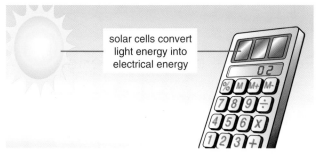

solar cells convert light energy into electrical energy

Figure 5 **A solar-powered calculator**

5 Biomass   The Sun's energy can be captured by plants and trees and turned into chemical energy which is released on burning. The trees and plants can then be replanted to capture even more of the Sun's energy.

Figure 6 **The burning of wood releases the stored energy**

6 Wave energy   The constant up and down movement of the surface of the sea can be used to generate electricity.

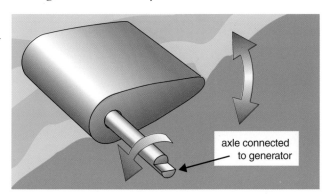

axle connected to generator

Figure 7 **Capturing wave energy**

Key terms

Check that you understand and can explain the following terms:

* energy resources
* fossil fuel
* renewable source
* non-renewable source
* fuel
* alternative sources of energy
* wind energy
* hydroelectric energy
* solar energy
* biomass
* tidal energy
* wave energy
* geothermal energy

Questions

1 Explain what is meant by the phrase 'non-renewable source of energy'. Give two examples of non-renewable sources of energy.

2 Explain what is meant by the phrase 'renewable source of energy'. Give two examples of renewable sources of energy.

3 Which renewable sources of energy depend upon the weather?

4 Which renewable sources of energy might be used in countries which a) have lots of mountains and hills, b) have lots of sunshine and c) have a coastline?

7 Geothermal energy   Deep inside the Earth it is very hot because of the radioactive materials which exist there. Cold water which is piped down into the ground returns as steam which can be used to generate electricity.

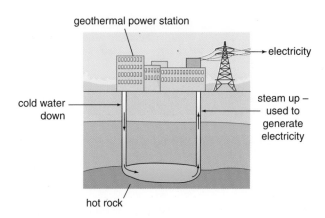

geothermal power station

→ electricity

cold water down

steam up – used to generate electricity

hot rock

Figure 8 **Capturing geothermal energy**

Generating electricity

Most of the electrical energy you use at home is **generated** at a power station.

Figure 1 **A fossil fuel power station**

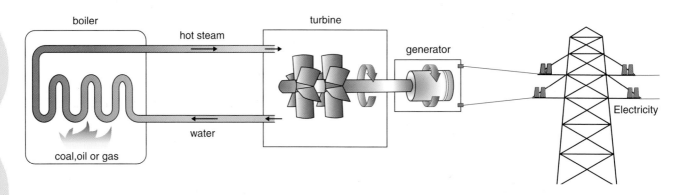

At a coal, oil or gas power station fuel is burned to produce heat energy. This heat energy is then used to change water into steam.

The energy contained in the steam is used to turn the **turbines**.

The turbines turn the generators which produce the electricity.

The electrical energy produced travels along a network of wires called the **National Grid** to your home.

The energy changes involved in this process are:

CHEMICAL ENERGY $\longrightarrow$ HEAT ENERGY $\longrightarrow$ KINETIC ENERGY $\longrightarrow$ ELECTRICAL ENERGY

At a nuclear power station the heat energy needed to produce the steam comes from radioactive materials such as uranium.

In a hydroelectric power station there is no boiler or steam. It is the kinetic energy of the water which is used to drive the turbines.

Figure 2 **A hydroelectric power station**

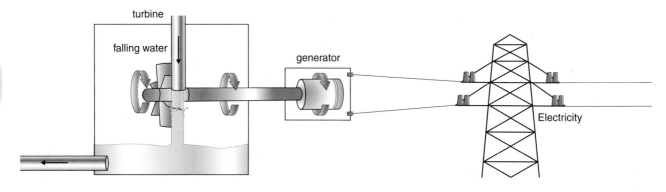

The energy changes involved are:

POTENTIAL ENERGY $\longrightarrow$ KINETIC ENERGY $\longrightarrow$ ELECTRICAL ENERGY

ENERGY AND ENERGY RESOURCES

Using energy from the Sun

The Sun is the main source of nearly all the different energy resources we use.

Figure 3 **This solar furnace in France captures energy from the Sun**

Key terms

Check that you understand and can explain the following terms:

★ generated
★ turbines
★ National Grid
★ energy chain
★ weather machine

★ biomass
★ carnivore
★ gravitational pull
★ tidal barrier

Questions

1   Name three fuels that might be burned at a power station.

2   Draw a block diagram to show the energy changes that take place at a power station.

3   Explain what is meant by the sentence, 'The Sun is the ultimate source of energy for the Earth'.

4   Name two energy sources that depend upon the 'weather machine'.

5   Explain where the energy in a piece of meat comes from.

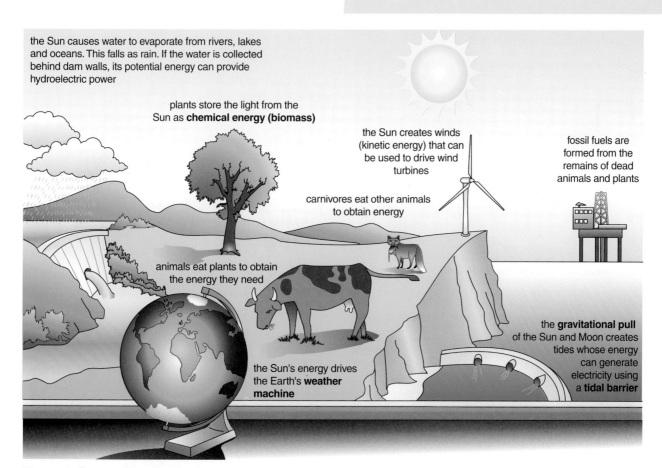

the Sun causes water to evaporate from rivers, lakes and oceans. This falls as rain. If the water is collected behind dam walls, its potential energy can provide hydroelectric power

plants store the light from the Sun as **chemical energy (biomass)**

the Sun creates winds (kinetic energy) that can be used to drive wind turbines

carnivores eat other animals to obtain energy

fossil fuels are formed from the remains of dead animals and plants

animals eat plants to obtain the energy they need

the Sun's energy drives the Earth's **weather machine**

the **gravitational pull** of the Sun and Moon creates tides whose energy can generate electricity using a **tidal barrier**

Figure 4 **Energy from the Sun creates useful energy resources**

What you need to know!

1 We need energy to live, to grow and to work.

2 There are several different forms of energy, including thermal energy, light energy, sound energy, electrical energy, chemical energy, nuclear energy, potential energy and kinetic energy.

3 When energy is used it changes into a different and more dilute form of energy.

4 Coal, oil and gas are fossil fuels.

5 Fossil fuels are non-renewable sources of energy.

6 Non-renewable sources of energy cannot be replaced once they have been used.

7 The energy contained in a fuel is released when it is burned.

8 Wind, hydroelectric energy, waves, tides, geothermal energy, solar energy and biomass are all renewable sources of energy.

9 Renewable sources of energy can be replaced.

10 The ultimate source of most of the Earth's energy is the Sun.

11 Electricity is generated at power stations using a variety of energy resources.

How much do you know?

1 The table below contains some examples of energy resources.

Tick the correct box to show whether an energy resource is renewable or non-renewable.

Energy resource	Renewable	Non-renewable
Coal		
Wind		
Solar		
Oil		
Gas		
Hydroelectric		

6 marks

2 a) A torch battery contains energy. In what form is this energy stored? Tick the correct box.

☐ light energy
☐ kinetic energy
☐ chemical energy
☐ electrical energy

1 mark

b) When the torch is turned on, energy flows from the battery to the bulb. In what form does the energy flow? Tick the correct box.

☐ light energy
☐ chemical energy
☐ electrical energy
☐ heat or thermal energy

c) Fill in the missing words to explain what energy change takes place in the bulb.

The bulb changes _____ energy into _____ energy and _____ energy.

3 marks

3 The diagram below shows a girl diving into a swimming pool.

How much do you know? continued

a) What kind of energy does the diver possess when she is standing on the board?

_____
1 mark

b) What kind of energy does the diver have just before she hits the water?

_____
1 mark

c) Where does all the diver's energy go after she has finished her dive?

_____
1 mark

4 a) Coal, oil and gas are fossil fuels. Explain briefly how they are formed.

_____

_____

_____
3 marks

b) Why are these fuels described as non-renewable energy resources?

_____

_____
2 marks

c) How is the energy released from a fuel?

_____
1 mark

d) Where does the energy stored in fossil fuels originally come from?

_____
1 mark

5 The diagram below is a block diagram of a coal-fired power station. Fill in the gaps in the diagram to show the energy changes that are taking place. The first one has been done for you.

	Boiler	Turbines	Generators
CHEMICAL ENERGY →	_____ →	_____ →	_____

3 marks

6 a) The Sun is the 'ultimate source of the Earth's energy resources'. Explain how the energy from the Sun became stored in the water behind the dam shown below.

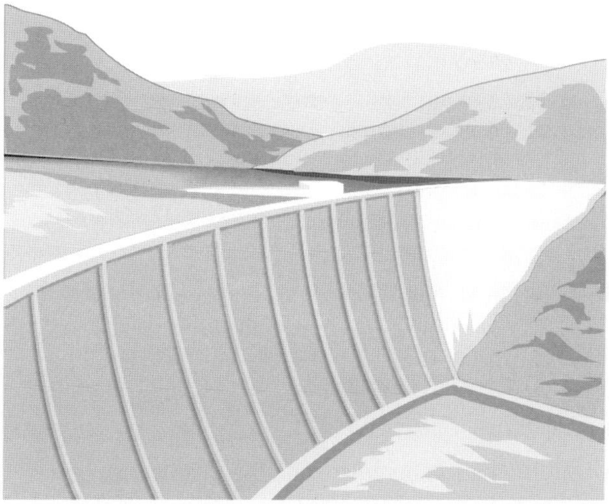

_____

_____

_____

_____
3 marks

b) What kind of energy is stored in the water?

_____
1 mark

c) Explain briefly how this energy can be changed into electrical energy.

_____

_____

_____
4 marks

LIFE PROCESSES & LIVING THINGS

Life Processes and Cells – pages 13–14

1 Feed, breathe, move and excrete *(4 marks)*

2 a) Nucleus – controls the activities in the cell *(1 mark)*
b) Cell membrane – holds the cell together / allows food and oxygen to enter the cell / allows waste products to leave the cell *(1 mark)*

3 a) Chloroplasts – absorb light energy so that the plant can make food *(1 mark)*
b) Cell wall – holds the plant together / gives support *(1 mark)*

Humans as Organisms (1) – pages 22–23

1 a) Bread and potatoes *(2 marks)*
b) Meat *(1 mark)*
c) Fibre helps to keep the digestive system clean and healthy *(1 mark)*

2 a) Not enough fibre – constipation
b) Not enough calcium – weak teeth and bones
c) Too much fat – heart disease
d) Not enough protein – poor growth
e) Not enough carbohydrate – lacking energy *(5 marks)*

3 a) To break them down into simpler substances In your mouth
b) Enzymes speed up 'digestive' reactions
c) In the small intestine *(4 marks)*

4 Capillaries, arteries, veins *(3 marks)*

5 a) The biceps contracts and the triceps relaxes
b) The biceps relaxes and the triceps contracts *(2 marks)*

Humans as Organisms (2) – pages 32–33

1 a) One every 28 days
b) In the Fallopian tubes
c) It passes out of the body *(3 marks)*

2 a) Food and oxygen
b) The inhaled smoke may harm her unborn baby *(2 marks)*

3 Any three from:

Boys – voice becomes deeper, hair grows on face and chest, become more muscular

Girls – breasts enlarge, begin periods, hair grows around pubic regions *(3 marks)*

4 a) Carbon dioxide *(1 mark)*
b) Oxygen *(1 mark)*
c) Smoking affects the lungs making it more difficult for the exchange of gases, especially when the energy demand is high *(2 marks)*

5 Oxygen and glucose *(2 marks)*

6 a) Any two diseases such as measles, mumps, chickenpox, polio, typhoid, etc. *(2 marks)*
b) Any two from: breathing them in, touching, being bitten, eating contaminated food. *(2 marks)*
c) White blood cells search out and kill invading germs *(2 marks)*
d) Vaccination prepares your immune system and strengthens your defences *(2 marks)*

Green Plants – pages 38–39

1 a) A, C, B *(3 marks)*
b) Part B attracts insects *(1 mark)*
c) Part C is the female part of the plant / contains the ovaries *(1 mark)*

2 a) Anther, pollination *(2 marks)*
b) By the wind *(1 mark)*
c) Pollen *(1 mark)*
d) Ovule *(1 mark)*

3 a) B, A, C, D *(4 marks)*
b) Leaves, fruit, roots, petals *(4 marks)*

4 a) Water + carbon dioxide + sunlight → food + oxygen *(5 marks)*
b) The tent has stopped the light reaching the grass so no photosynthesis has taken place *(3 marks)*
c) Photosynthesis takes place and the grass becomes green again *(2 marks)*
d) The grass would die *(1 mark)*

5 a) Food + oxygen → carbon dioxide + water + energy *(5 marks)*
b) Respiration *(1 mark)*
c) It is stored by the plant *(1 mark)*

6 a) Oxygen and carbon dioxide *(2 marks)*
b) Water *(1 mark)*

Variation, Classification and Inheritance – pages 44–45

1 C, B, A, D *(4 marks)*

2 Dandelion – A, lion – C, jellyfish – D, carrot – B, tulip – A, monkey – C, worm – D, human – C *(8 marks)*

3 a) Discontinuous variation *(1 mark)*
   b) It is a characteristic at least one of your parents
      has *(1 mark)*
   c) B and 2 *(2 marks)*

Living Things in the Environment – pages 52– 53

1 a) Aphids or caterpillars, blue tits and great tits
      (2 marks)
   b) Wood mice, weasels *(2 marks)*
   c) Oak tree *(1 mark)*
   d) Caterpillars, weasels, wood mice, blue tits, great
      tits or sparrowhawks *(1 mark)*

2 a) Rabbits,
   b) Blue tits
   c) The number of foxes will decrease
   d) The number of rabbits will increase *(4 marks)*

3 a) The slug population decreases
   b) The plant population increases
   c) The plant population increases because there are
      fewer slugs *(3 marks)*

4 a) Owl
   b) Curlew
   c) Woodpecker
   d) Swift *(4 marks)*

5 Any two from: has a thick coat to keep warm, white
   coat for camouflage, long claws to catch prey, big
   paws to avoid sinking into snow, hibernates in the
   winter *(2 marks)*

MATERIALS & THEIR PROPERTIES

Classifying Materials (1) – pages 60–61

1 a) Oxygen, b) iron, c) iron, d) oxygen, e) iron,
   f) water and oxygen *(7 marks)*

2 a) Liquid, b) liquid, c) solid, d) gas, e) solid,
   f) C and E *(7 marks)*

3 a) Between B and C, X is melting *(1 mark)*
   b) Between D and E, X is boiling *(1 mark)*
   c) Between C and D, the particles in X are able to
      move around a little but are still held together by
      weak forces.
   d) No forces – gas; very strong forces – solid.
      (2 marks)

4 a) Any two elements close to Na in the periodic table
      e.g. lithium or potassium *(2 marks)*
   b) Any two elements close to Ne in the periodic table
      e.g. helium or argon *(2 marks)*
   c) Hydrogen has 1 proton, sodium has 11 protons,
      carbon has 6 protons *(3 marks)*

Classifying Materials (2) – pages 70–71

1 Heat the coffee/water solution in order to boil away
   the water and leave the coffee powder behind.
   (2 marks)

2 a) The sand is left in the filter paper. *(1 mark)*
   b) The salt passes through the filter paper into the
      beaker *(1 mark)*
   c) Both salt and sugar will dissolve in water, so both
      would pass through the filter paper *(2 marks)*

3 a) At 78°C the alcohol boils and travels up and along
      the condenser *(1 mark)*
   b) As the alcohol vapour travels through the
      condenser, it is cooled and changes back into a
      liquid *(1 mark)*

4 a) Pen C *(1 mark)*
   b) The chromatography tests showed that this pen
      contained ink which was identical to that which
      was used to write the false cheque *(2 marks)*

5 a) A compound
   b) A solution or a mixture
   c) A chemical change *(3 marks)*

6 Properties of a metal – strong, flexible, shiny, good
   conductor of heat

   Properties of a non-metal – brittle, low melting point,
   low density, poor conductor of electricity *(8 marks)*

7 Carbon dioxide CO_2; water H_2O *(2 marks)*

Changing Materials (1) – pages 78–79

1 a) Takes in; remains the same *(2 marks)*
   b) Gives out; remains the same *(2 marks)*

2 a) The ice is melting
   b) The water is boiling
   c) B
   d) C *(4 marks)*

3 Warm the solution; stir the solution *(2 marks)*

4 a) As the ball is heated it expands and becomes too
      big to pass through the ring *(2 marks)*
   b) As the ball cools it contracts and so can pass
      through the ring once more *(2 marks)*

5 A – sedimentary, B – metamorphic, C – igneous,
   D – metamorphic *(4 marks)*

6 a) Bottom left label – deposition; top label –
      transport; middle right label – melting *(3 marks)*
   b) High pressure and high temperature *(2 marks)*

Changing Materials (2) – pages 86–87

1 Natural materials – stone, slate

   Man-made materials – brick, glass, concrete,
   aluminium, steel, plastic   (8 marks)

2 Iron ore – steel, wood – paper, clay – brick, flour –
   bread, oil – plastic   (5 marks)

3 a) Nail C   (1 mark)
   b) Any two from: coat nail surface with paint, grease,
       plastic or non-corroding metal   (2 marks)

4 Heating the ingredients of a cake in an oven
   Grilling some bread to make toast
   Burning gas on a stove   (3 marks)

5 Oxygen; carbon dioxide   (2 marks)

6 A – nothing happens to limewater
   B – splint continues to burn
   C – limewater turns milky
   D – splint goes out
   E – nothing happens to limewater
   F – hydrogen burns with a 'pop'   (6 marks)

7 a) The gas in Bunsen burner A is completely burnt.
       The flame from Bunsen burner A is therefore
       hotter than that of Bunsen burner B.   (2 marks)
   b) It will become covered with soot (carbon).   (1 mark)

Patterns of Behaviour – pages 96–97

1 Most reactive B   D   C   A Least reactive (4 marks)

2 a) Calcium – fairly quick reaction with quite a few
       bubbles of gas being released
       Copper – no reaction at all, no bubbles of gas
       released
   b) Hydrogen
   c) Because copper does not react with water
   d) Carbon dioxide
   e) Calcium sulphate   (6 marks)

3 a) Rust or iron oxide   (1 mark)
   b) Oxidation reaction   (1 mark)
   c) Iron + water $\rightarrow$ iron oxide + hydrogen (4 marks)
   d) Iron   (1 mark)

4 a) Oven spray
   b) Vinegar
   c) Fresh milk
   d) Vinegar   (4 marks)

5 a) Purple
   b) Red
   c) Alkaline
   d) 7   (4 marks)

PHYSICAL PROCESSES

Electricity – pages 106–107

1 The plastic rod and the cloth   (2 marks)

2 a) A
   b) C
   c) B   (3 marks)

3 a) Negative

   b) Some negative charges have been rubbed off the
       balloon and onto John's jumper.   (2 marks)

4 a) Because the circuit was incomplete, i.e. there was
       a gap in the wires.   (1 mark)
   b) The key and the coin   (2 marks)
   c) Both objects are made of metal. Metals are good
       conductors of electricity.   (2 marks)

5 a) B   (1 mark)
   b) D   (1 mark)
   c) A and C   (2 marks)

6 Because in the circuit containing bulb B, the cells are
   not connected correctly and the current cannot flow.

7 The charges can flow more easily through the piece
   of copper wire than through the resistor.   (2 marks)

Electricity and Magnetism – pages 112–113

1 a) A and B   (2 marks)
   b) B and C   (2 marks)
   c) This will happen because the current takes the
       path of least resistance, i.e. it is easier for the
       current to pass through the wire than through the
       bulb.   (2 marks)

2 Place the north pole of magnet 1 next to one of the
   poles of magnet 2. If the magnets repel, the
   unknown pole is a north pole. If they attract, the
   unknown pole of magnet 2 is a south pole.   (3 marks)

3 The following statements are true:
   A magnet will attract an iron rod.
   A magnet will not attract a piece of wood.

                                                    (2 marks)

4 When the button is pressed, current flows around the
   electromagnet i.e. the electromagnet is turned on. It
   attracts the iron rod causing the hammer to hit the
   bell.   (2 marks)

5 a) 0.1 A   (1 mark)
   b) 0.2 A   (1 mark)
   c) The current flowing through Ammeter 1 will be
       larger than that in circuit 1.   (1 mark)

6 a) A has a series lighting circuit.   (1 mark)
   b) B has a parallel lighting circuit   (2 marks)

Forces and Motion – pages 124–125

1 a) He goes faster *(1 mark)*
b) Speed = distance / time = 40 m / 8 s
= 5 m/s *(2 marks)*

2 a) 10 minutes *(1 mark)*
b) 4 m/s *(1 mark)*
c) 5 minutes *(1 mark)*

3 a) The wagon would slow down *(1 mark)*
The wagon would travel at a constant speed *(1 mark)*

4 The ball has changed shape. *(1 mark)*

5 a) Moment = distance × force = 0.5 m ×
50 N = 25 Nm *(3 marks)*
b) Use a longer spanner *(1 mark)*

6 John should move back to the end of the see-saw *(2 marks)*

7 a) The girl wearing the snowshoes creates less pressure on the snow and so does not sink. The girl without the snowshoes creates a large pressure on the snow and so sinks *(3 marks)*

Pressure = force / area = 500 N / 0.5 m^2
= 1000 Pa *(2 marks)*

Light and Sound – pages 134–135

1 The blindfold prevents light reflected by the other people from entering the boy's eyes *(2 marks)*

2 B *(1 mark)*

4 a) A spectrum or the colours of the rainbow *(1 mark)*
b) Just red light *(1 mark)*

5 Light waves travel much faster than sound waves *(2 marks)*

6 a) Strike the gong harder *(1 mark)*
b) The larger bell *(1 mark)*

7 a) It may become damaged *(1 mark)*
b) Don't listen to the music so often and turn down the volume / loudness of the music. *(2 marks)*

Earth in Space – pages 142–143

1 a) The letter B should be written in circle directly above the tree *(1 mark)*
b) The letter C should be written in the last circle on the right *(1 mark)*
c) The circle should be drawn directly below the circle which you have marked B *(1 mark)*

2 a) A and B *(2 marks)*
b) C and D *(2 marks)*
c) A *(1 mark)*

3 a) The letter A should be put in the box on the right *(1 mark)*
b) The letter B should be put in the box on the left *(1 mark)*

4 a) Pluto
b) Mercury
c) Jupiter
d) Pluto
e) Mercury
f) Mercury *(7 marks)*

5 a) Planets, Sun, orbits *(3 marks)*
b) Galaxy *(1 mark)*
c) Luminous; moons; reflect *(3 marks)*

6 B, A, C, F, D, E *(5 marks)*

Energy and Energy Resources – pages 150–151

1 Renewable – wind, solar, hydroelectric
Non-renewable – coal, oil, gas *(6 marks)*

2 a) Chemical energy *(1 mark)*
b) Electrical energy *(1 mark)*
c) Electrical energy, heat energy and light energy *(3 marks)*

3 a) Potential energy
b) Kinetic energy
c) To heat or thermal energy *(3 marks)*

4 a) Plants and animals die and become covered with lots of layers of mud. The high pressures and temperatures change the dead plants and animals into coal, oil or gas *(3 marks)*
b) Once they have been used up they cannot be replaced *(2 marks)*
c) By burning *(1 mark)*
d) The Sun *(1 mark)*

5 Heat energy, kinetic energy, electrical energy *(3 marks)*

6 a) Heat energy from the Sun warms the water. It evaporates, rises and gains potential energy. When it rains, the water is collected behind the dam before it can return to the sea *(3 marks)*
b) Potential energy *(1 mark)*
c) The water is allowed to flow out and down from the dam. As the water flows it turns turbines. The turbines turn generators. The generators produce electrical energy *(4 marks)*